Celebrating Parenting

AF673329

Celebrating Parenting

Shabnam Gupta

PRABHAT
PRAKASHAN

No part of this publication can be reproduced, stored in a retrieval system or transmitted in any form or by any means, electronic, mechanical, photocopying, recording or otherwise, without the prior permission of the author and the publisher.

Published by
PRABHAT PRAKASHAN PVT. LTD.
4/19 Asaf Ali Road,
New Delhi-110 002 (INDIA)
e-mail: prabhatbooks@gmail.com

ISBN 978-93-5186-674-9
CELEBRATING PARENTING
by Shabnam Gupta

© Reserved

Edition
2025

Price
₹ 200.00 (Rupees Two Hundred only)

Printed at
R-Tech Offset Printers, Delhi

Your children are not your children.

They are the sons and daughters of Life's longing for itself.

They come through you but not from you,

And though they are with you, yet they belong not to you.

You may give them your love but not your thoughts.

For they have their own thoughts.

You may house their bodies but not their souls,

For their souls dwell in the house of tomorrow, which you cannot visit, not even in your dreams.

You may strive to be like them, but seek not to make them like you.

For life goes not backward nor tarries with yesterday.

You are the bows from which your children as living arrows are sent forth.

The archer sees the mark upon the path of the infinite, and He bends you with His might that His arrows may go swift and far.

Let your bending in the archer's hand be for gladness;

For even as He loves the arrow that flies, so He loves also the bow that is stable.

—Kahlil Gibran

Author's Note

About 15 years back, as a young mother, I was always overwhelmed. And fearful. I had so many questions, and no answers. Of course, Dr. Benjamin Spock, Adele Faber and their ilk held my hand for a while, but could not assuage my fears. Not totally. I read the best books on parenting, written by trained child psychologists, Ph.Ds. and M.Ds., but there was only one problem. They were speaking to the Western world. I needed to hear from someone who knew my world, my challenges, my insecurities and my social milieu. I missed that. The network of friends, relatives and older mothers helped, but I missed having a book by my bedside, which was written for me, which I could leaf through and find answers.

The fear which almost immobilized me at most times was that, as a mother, I was handling a real, living human being. Who could be hurt or harmed by my ignorance or neglect. And the harm may not always be physical, or visible. With such an attitude, I forgot to enjoy the biggest blessing of my life – being a parent.

But, even then, I knew it wasn't right. Love is not enough, insight is insufficient, parents need direction and a certain set of skills.

This is how this book came about.

I'm not a Parenting Expert. In fact, I'm not sure that I even believe that an expert can teach Parenting. I'm an involved, constantly learning, hands-on parent, and like most of you, I'm also learning on the job.

—Shabnam Gupta

Preface

An Internet Message—

The young mother set her foot on the path of life, "Is this way long?" she asked. And the guide said: "Yes, and the way is hard. And you will be old before you reach the end of it. But the end will be better than the beginning." But the young mother was happy and she would not believe that anything could be better than these years.

So she played with her children, and gathered flowers for them along the way, and bathed them in the clear streams, and the sun shone on them and the young mother cried, "Nothing will ever be lovelier than this."

Then the night came, and the storm, and the path was dark, and the children shook with fear and cold, and the mother drew them close and covered them with her mantle, and the children said, "Mother, we are not afraid, for you are near, and no harm can come."

And the morning came, and there was a hill ahead, and the children climbed and grew weary, and the mother was exhausted.

But, at all times, she said to the children, "A little patience and we are there." So, the children climbed, and when they reached the top, they said, "Mother, we could not have done it without you."

And the mother, when she lay down at night, looked up at the stars and said, "This is a better day than the last, for my children have learned fortitude in the face of hardness. Yesterday I gave them courage, today I've given them strength."

And the next day came strange clouds which darkened the earth, clouds of war and hate and evil, and the children groped and stumbled, and the mother said, "Look up. Lift your eyes to the light."

And the children looked and saw above the clouds an everlasting glory, and it guided them beyond the darkness. And the mother said, "This is the best day of all, for I have shown my children God."

And the days went on, and the weeks, months and the years, and the mother grew old and frail and bent.

But her children were tall and strong and walked with courage. And when the way was rough, they lifted her for she was as light as feather; and at last when they came to a hill beyond, they could see a shining road and golden gates flung wide.

And the mother said, "I have reached the end of my journey. And now I know that the end is better than the beginning, for my children can walk alone, and their children after them."

And the children said, "You will always walk with us, mother, even when you have gone through the gates."

And they stood and watched her as she went alone, and the gates closed after her. And they said, "We cannot see her, but she is with us still. A mother like ours is more than a memory. She is a living presence."

It is a beautiful story. Substitute Parents for Mother, and you have a perfect parable for the journey of parenthood.

For journey it is.

But every journey needs forethought, planning and investment.

Contents

Parenting as a Conscious Choice

Parenting is the only job in the world which is given without any qualifications, skill or training. It is not even taken as a serious job in our country for the simple reason that it comes about effortlessly, and is accepted as a natural progression of life's evolution. The life plan of an average Indian, both for himself and for his children, consists of four major milestones: Study, get a job, marry, and have kids! No confusion, no controversy, no negotiation.

And, not enough thought, preparation or counselling is given to marriage or parenting. In fact, there is more attention to detail in the planning of the wedding ceremony, than to married life!

In an average Indian household (and we're talking about a cross-section of society here), when the parents feel that the child has reached a certain marriageable age (mostly 22-25 years for girls, and 24-28 years for boys), the proposals are sought, and the marriage finalized. Maturity level, career scene and individual preferences are taken into consideration, but only marginally. The only training a young bride or groom gets before setting foot into this holy institution is the model before him – his parents, his cousins, his friends and the immediate society around him. The only preparation he is required to do is give his consent, and the only advice given by the elders – *"ye to wo ladoo hai jo khata hai wo bhi rota hai, jo nahi khata hai wo bhi."*

With this mindset and groundwork, what we don't realize is that we've left a child, blindfolded, in a zone of landmines! Explosions are bound to happen.

Then comes parenthood. Again, aided and abetted by the not-so-subtle hints of parents and society around us. Again, age being the guiding criteria. Issues like preparedness and maturity aside, parenthood is decided by the age of the couple and number of married years.

And a couple of years later, the story repeats when parents put pressure on the couple for another child.

The whole concept is skewed. How can we not realize that these two institutions, marriage and parenthood, involve living human beings, not inanimate machines, and require both training and preparation? All 24-year-olds aren't intellectually, emotionally or financially the same and their maturity level is going to affect the lives, happiness and well-being of the people around them, then how can we not bother giving them correct guidelines or counselling sessions? Before handing over even one of our machines to a new worker, we ensure that he has the technical know-how to handle it, how then can we be so blind that we hand human being(s) over to a novice without making sure that he is capable enough to do so?

The task of bringing a child into this world, and bringing him up well, requires skills and a certain maturity. What we have here is another human being, a living life, whom we can either nurture or crush. The dents and trauma will not be visible, but it will have a lasting impact, sometimes down the generations, out of control and beyond repair.

After all, the damage done to humans is far more serious and irreparable.

Let's open our eyes to the magnitude of the task before us. Let ours be Responsible and Conscious Parenting. Let us *choose* parenthood, let us *choose* to be parents. Not have it thrust or forced upon us. When issues like financial planning, compatibility and stability in marriage are given due consideration, parenthood is the next logical step. Biological age is an important element here. And it is a very important factor in having, and raising, healthy progeny. Don't put off having children for too long. Plan children while you are still young enough to enjoy them and grow with them.

For you will need every ounce of energy to conceive, bear and then rear them.

□

Welcome Aboard

Parenting is a Marathon. Not a Sprint

First of all, realize this. Parenting does not have a time stamp, an expiry date. Once a parent, always a parent. So, don't take the short-term view.

Parenting does not Have to be Lonesome

Know that you are not alone in this. We parents are a confused, fearful and unsure lot who are always second guessing ourselves. Welcome to our world! Most of what we learn is by trial and error, and learnt along the way. But there are a few things that go a long way in helping us out.

Like knowing a few facts and remembering them at all times.

- Parenting is a two-way process. Children teach us more than we can teach them. We just have to adjust our antennas to their frequency.
- No two human beings are alike, so there is no rule that can be applied uniformly. You cannot have a one-size-fits-all rule when you

are dealing with something as diverse and ever-changing as the human race!

- The two main ingredients which take care of most of the parenting woes and dilemmas are love and instinct. The rest takes care of itself at most of the times.
- Family is a sacred commitment, the life-spring of our well-being, and it should be honoured as such. It is a delicate plant which needs to be nourished and nurtured every single day. It's not a pet whom you stroke absent-mindedly once in a while, and consider your duty done.
- Children do not need to be managed, or controlled, each child is unique and individual. It is futile to even attempt to try it.
- The best lessons parents can teach the children are by example, not by preaching them.
- Parenthood should be a choice – default vs. design. It should be something you want, not just the next milestone in your life plan.
- Children know when you do something out of sincerity and when it is just a lip talk. Pretending doesn't work.
- There's no such thing as right parenting and wrong parenting, and there's no such thing as a good parent or a bad parent.
- No two children are alike. Neither siblings, nor cousins, not even twins. So comparing lemons and oranges is a waste of breath.
- TV, Internet, cellphone are a necessary evil, they have invaded our worlds, and will

continue to do so. They are responsible for information overload as well as aspirational living.

- Parents cannot be perfect at all times, mistakes and lapses are bound to happen. But don't keep beating yourself about it. We are human, we make mistakes.

It takes a Village to Raise a Child

Understanding the Joint Family System in India

In India, the joint family has always been a part of our lives. In fact, we used to say that *Bachha kisi ek ka nahi hota, sanjha hota hai. Sanjha* – joint; where everyone contributes towards influencing and shaping of the child's personality.

The post-Partition (1947 onwards) Indian joint family usually meant grandparents, hordes of uncles, aunts and cousins mostly in the same house, eating out of the same kitchen, and co-existing in harmony. In fact, it was not even considered funny when a small child, when asked in school about how many brothers and sisters he had, would often count on his tiny fingers, and then proudly declare '51!' The teacher understood. Children, back then, genuinely did not know who their real siblings were and who the cousins were! In fact, almost all children of this generation have called their father "*chacha*", or whatever it was the eldest child in the family was calling him. Without realizing that his cousin's *chacha* was his father, and he should be addressing him as father!

On an average, it was customary for a couple to have a brood of 9-10 children then. Since infant mortality was quite high, mostly six or seven survived. Multiply this with six brothers of the father's generation, all living together, and you have a pretty big family!

The dynamics of this type of family were wide-ranging. The children were left pretty much to themselves, or to the older cousins' mercy. Parents were not involved in full time parenting. In fact, they never thought of parenting as a duty, or something that needed to be done. The mothers in such a set-up were a very busy lot, and their duties included cooking, cleaning, laundry, stitching, knitting and a host of other household chores which consumed all their time, attention and energies. This was all done alongside giving birth to a baby almost every year!

The menfolk went to work, and put food on the table. That was their role. Conversations, as we know them today, between parent and child, did not happen ever. Parents and other household elders were to be feared. Not fraternized with. Respect had shades of fear. Speaking in front of them was bad manners. 'Children were meant to be seen, not heard.' A big part of parental duties was considered to be ensuring that the children went to school, and punishing them when they didn't. And, of course, taking them to the doctor, as and when required.

And, this too was the assigned duty of one particular male member who took over this role. He was the father-figure for all the children in the family. He was not averse to whacking the children whenever he thought they needed it. His authority over them was absolute, and it wasn't questioned or challenged. All the children feared this uncle.

One big difference between parents of that era and parents of today is the complete confidence the elders had in those days. Whatever they did, they did with authority; whatever we do, we do it with hesitation. Even when they were wrong, they acted with sureness; even when we are right, we act with doubt.

The biggest advantage of growing up in this type of a big joint family was that a child's social and interpersonal skills were tested and polished on home turf itself. Living with diverse personalities and different age groups brought about a degree of tolerance and acceptance, and having to deal with lack of personalized attention, bullying by older cousins and strict discipline brought about a degree of resilience in the child's personality. Since there was no one to run to with stories of insults and hurts, they learnt to deal with it themselves. More or less, the security and safety of the child was not a big challenge, since there were more than enough adults around to keep an eye on him. Creches and day-care centers were unheard of in those days.

Slowly, over the time, this concept started changing, and somewhere around the 1980s, the line between real and cousins started being drawn more clearly. Social historians will be able to highlight the macro consequences of this shift, but the real setback was the breakdown of the family unit from joint to nuclear set up. Uncles, aunts and cousins moved out, and only real siblings remained in the same house. The family size started shrinking. The number of children per couple came down to three.

With cousins out of the scene, and sisters getting married and moving to their own houses, the next step towards family division came between the brothers. Once the brothers grew up, they moved away and set up houses of their own.

Post-1990s, in an average Indian household, it is just the parents and the children which make up a family. And a posse of servants.

Changes have come about, and we have to accept these changes. It is no use wishing that things could go back to being as they were. We have to become conscious about how they affect our lives, and learn to deal with it.

The Happy Indian Joint Family Today

Today, the Indian joint family means husband's parents, an unmarried sister or brother, or both. Relatives are a social support system, and family ties are duly honoured. The only change is that though we are not living with them in the same house, uncles, aunts and cousins still play a very active and important role in our lives. Staying in touch via telephone, messaging and regular socializing ensures closer bonds.

And compromise on a lot of fronts. At least when it comes to child rearing. Advice on how to feed, bathe, burp the baby aside, a new mother is bombarded with well-meaning relatives and elders who confuse her with homespun theories, and often conflicting advice. It becomes a challenge for the new mother to balance the feelings of family members with her own sensibility and instinct. Constant refrains of family seniors being, 'As if we haven't brought up children' or 'These new-fangled theories don't mean your doctor knows more than us.'

They have more hands-on experience, true, but this is your child, and hence your right and privilege to bring him up the way you want to.

The important thing here is to strike a balance, take their well-meaning advice with a pinch of respect for their experience, and then doing what you think is right for your child. Remember, no two children are the same. Your child is not the same as his father, or even his own sibling. And no one, except you, his parent, can know better. Which means that no one can feed, or treat your child, in any way which is not acceptable to you.

The key here is to be firm, but polite, about your parenting do's and dont's. There is no reason to disregard a good piece of advice, but there is also no reason to be a mute spectator in your own child's life.

The Challenges Indian Nuclear Family Today

Then there is the nuclear set up. In the last 15 years, urban India, especially in the metros, has seen more of working couples living on their own, with their children, but without their own parents or siblings. These couples have migrated from small towns in search of livelihood to metros like Delhi, Mumbai, Bangalore, etc. They face challenges like culture shock along with their displacement woes, and find it difficult to bring up their children with the same sensibility with which they themselves were brought up. They want to, but they realize that they cannot. There's a definite sense of losing touch with their intrinsic values, and a fear that they might totally get disconnected from their roots. This conflict, coupled with the fact that they now have servants looking after their children, instead of family members, means that exposure to the native family culture has to become a conscious process. A part of the parenting process.

Even for the families where one parent, mostly the mother, is staying at home to bring up the children, the same challenges persist. Lifestyles have changed. Mothers have an active social life, both outside and inside the house. The focus has turned on to oneself – 'me-time', 'privacy' and 'space', have become acceptable concepts in our lives, and women have the choice to pursue hobbies and interests. She's entitled to her evening out with friends, or an evening in with friends. It is acceptable if she leaves her children in the care of an *ayah* while she goes for her Kathak class! It is no longer looked down upon.

But the shifting dynamics have brought about changes in parenting styles also. The concerns have changed, the challenges have multiplied. And family has shrunk. Support system has dwindled. We feel shy to ask for help. Our mothers feel shy to offer help, in the fear that they might be invading our 'space.' An escalation in accidents and crime in the recent years has also spelt defining changes in the upbringing of children. Children can no longer be unsupervised even for a few minutes. Young children cannot cycle down to the neighbourhood park on their own, or play on the road if there is no adult to supervise them. This means they have to be kept busy indoors with computers, laptops, television and telephones. And satellite television has brought the Western culture right inside our houses.

The demons we parents have to battle today, exist both outside and within. It's an uphill task, and fears of going wrong loom large.

Parenting needs to be redefined in this context. This will happen only when we acknowledge that parenting is an acquired skill, and given today's current scenario, it needs to be given serious and solemn thought.

Given that anxiety looms large on every parent's mind, there is always hope. Let us see if we can figure out a way together, and learn from each other's mistakes.

Let me begin by sharing my own experience.

My Daily Routine

Not long ago, my day started with waking up my four-year-old, my primary focus being to get her to school on time, so I could get on with the rest of my day.

Looking back now I realize, it was actually quite bizarre.

I would keep asking her to hurry up even when I could see that she was trying her best. There was no time for tenderness, I just yanked off her clothes, pushed her into the bathroom, rushed her through a hasty bath, gave her no time to linger or enjoy, combed her hair, and mentally ticked off each item against an ironclad, non-negotiable checklist. Hair – check; shoes – check; tiffin – check; bag – check; and water bottle – check and so on. Then I would rush her into the car, drive like a maniac, zipping through the traffic to make it to school on time, not making any conversation other than cursing everyone who came in my way.

Once I reached the school, I cursed some more, since there was never any parking space close to the school gate. Then I would walk her down to the gate, give her an absent-minded hug, and hand her over to the teacher, even while the to-do list for the day had already started playing in my mind. This went on for a few months. I am so ashamed of it, but it did.

Till one day, as I was coursing through the traffic at my usual breakneck speed, I happened to glance in the rear view mirror and saw my child's eyes –

frightened and unhappy. Her mouth was in a droop, and her shoulders were slumped. It was a sorry sight, believe me. It shook me. My rash driving coupled with my angry demeanor had frightened her. My happy, cheerful, smiling baby had turned into this! And I was the one responsible for turning her into this sad little thing.

The realization hit me like a blast of cold water. Something happened, I knew I had been the jerk here. And, it needed to be corrected. Right at that very moment.

I slowed down, put on some music, took a deep breath, smiled, and started talking to her. About school, about her friends, about our dog. Slowly, I watched her relax, a small smile fluttered on her face and her eyes started dancing. Just the way I liked them to.

I saw a different child then.

And realized my mistake.

Punctuality is important, and has to be followed and enforced, but it doesn't have to be so stressful. Efficient planning and a relaxed attitude can make it a pleasant habit. I was making it stressful for myself and my child, and my attitude had turned me into a witch with a broomstick in my child's eyes.

That day, I made a few promises to myself.

□

Promises to Keep

What is our long-term goal as parents? We want to raise happy and healthy children. And we want to open doors for them to learn, connect and grow through good academics, healthy relationships and satisfying hobbies. Children who grow up to be responsible and successful adults, and who contribute towards society.

What do we do to get there?

Relax, take a few breaths, smile often.

Let smiles and joy walk with parenthood, not guilt and regret.

The first promise I made to myself was to try and be as relaxed and calm as possible. This meant streamlining and re-prioritizing my life. I had to decide what was more important. Given that I still had to get my child ready for school on time, my focus shifted from sending a perfectly dressed and groomed baby to sending a happy, cheerful baby to school.

Children pick up energy and vibes, tone and signals from the parents, and I didn't want to be transmitting negative energy any more. Not now when I'd become aware of my mistake. I started getting up fifteen minutes before time, and sipping a leisurely cup of tea before waking up my daughter. Then a few minutes of hug time, and we'd be ready to start our day.

It didn't happen in a day. I had to constantly keep shutting off the voices in my head, and slowing down my inner clock to keep up with my child without being late.

I tried to keep a smile on my face, I spoke softly, more lovingly when I had to ask her to hurry up, and most importantly, I started asking her what she wanted to do. It meant making changes, some days she'd want me to comb her hair, on others she'd want to take a bath after school, not in the morning. This meant that my mornings could not have a fixed, predictable structure or routine. It meant that I had to go off-script very often.

But that was it.

The only adjustment was that my mornings never had the same drab drill every day. Each morning was different from the previous.

And required me to write late-note more often, I grant you that!

But we were enjoying ourselves. Oh! yes, we were smiling more, singing more often and feeling happier.

The drive to the school became an exclusive 'us-time.' Mostly we talked and sang, sometimes we were silent. We started getting clued-in to each other's moods: we could make out which silence was angry, and which was sad; when we wanted to talk, and when we didn't.

My most stressful time of the day had suddenly become the most beautiful part, and I didn't want to trade it for anything else.

What it had required was just an awareness and re-prioritization.

Relaxation Tips

- Waking up 15 minutes before time.
- Make preparation the night before a habit.
- Deep breathing every morning for at least five minutes.
- Try to see the bigger picture, not the small frame in front of you. It will put things in the right perspective. You may rush your child to school today and make it on time, but will she remember what she was about to talk to you when you rudely asked her to, 'hurry up, or we'll be late.'
- Ask yourself every now and then: It's important to reach on time, but isn't it equally important to smell the flowers on the way?
- Remind yourself every now and then that parenthood is a blessing. Reserved for the fortunate.

Watch What You Say and How You Say It

My next promise to myself was that I would talk

to my child with the politeness and civility that I reserved for friends. As parents, we talk down to them, thinking they don't understand and appreciate the difference. They do. And it's important to them.

Children learn what they live. If they live with understanding and compassion, they learn to respect. If they live with criticism, they learn to doubt themselves and others, they distrust the intentions of those around them.

In India, we still don't think of our children as individuals. We think of them merely as our shadows, or extensions, who don't deserve our respect.

But they are individuals in their own right. They have a keen sense of self-respect, and feel belittled when you ignore or brush them aside. Keeping in mind these little points will help:

- Don't patronize children or talk down to them.
- Keep a soft and pleasant tenor in your voice when talking to your child, like you have when you talk to a friend.
- Do not try to put off answering his questions. They may not be important to you, but they are important to him.
- Be honest. Tell him if you don't know the answer. Suggest that you look for the answer together.
- Do not brush their opinion, fears or concerns aside without considering them. Listen. Show

them that what they say, matters. Reinforce their faith in their own voice.

Pay Attention without Distraction

My next promise to myself was to pay attention to my child. Undivided sincere attention. Not pretend to pay attention.

In our agenda-laden lives, there is always a rush to tick items off our lists. Our lives are managed and controlled by electronic devices, especially our phones and laptops, and they've become our extended arms and our lungs. We hang on to them as if our lives depended on it. And we are running on schedules. Tight, well-planned schedules.

There are *external* distractions, like phones, laptops, I-pads, endless lists, calendars and appointments. Then there are *internal* distractions like pressure to look picture perfect at all times, need to stick to ironclad schedules, suitability and convenience, dislike of disorganized masses – these take away from the fun and spontaneity of the moment and dictate our choices.

So, what happens?

The first price we pay for our over-packed, gadget controlled lives is the childhood of our children.

When we are not conscious of this, what do we normally do? Our phones are on at all times of the day, and it's ring and beep always gets our first attention.

The first thing we do on getting up in the morning is check our phones, not hug or greet our family. An everyday scenario all around us in a museum, a movie hall, our child's school function or even the doctor's clinic, parents who are busy on their phones, or other online activity, while their children look longingly at them. And when the child does start talking to them, they respond with an absent-minded grunt at best, or brush off the child rudely with a 'Not now, honey. I'm busy.' The caller, who is miles away, gets more importance than our child sitting in front of us with his building blocks.

At red lights, we maximize our productivity by reading and answering emails and texts. Hands-free bluetooth receivers mean that we can converse even when we are driving. Regardless of the fact that our children are sitting in the car with us, and we could use that time not only to talk and listen to them with undivided attention, but also set an example of safe driving to them. It has now been researched and proved that accidents happen not because one was holding the phone and talking, but because of reduced attention and slower reflexes due to the conversation. So hands-free or not, if you are talking and driving, you are inviting trouble.

- Pay sincere and genuine attention to your child.
- Work is important, so are games on our phones. But children are far more important.
- Cut down on distractions, put the phone on

silent mode every now and then. That option is there for a reason.

- Use driving time as 'us-time', with your children, and make it as fun and technology free as possible.

We Teach more by What We Do, Than by What We Say

It is a fact that children will learn more from they *see*, than from what they *hear*.

And what do they see?

Parents busy on phones, computers or any other screen or monitor. Talking, texting, chatting, or even playing games.

Yes. Forget work, even the games on the computer screen have become more important than going out cycling, swimming or swinging the bat with our child.

Since when did virtual life start taking over the real one?

This was the most difficult realization for me. It was the same story everywhere I looked. Technology has overpowered every waking minute of our lives. Phones are an extension of our hands, we feel lost without them.

Do we realize the missed opportunities here? The chances we have lost of being with our children, of connecting with them and being with them in the present moment?

Yes, that's the way the world is nowadays, and gadgets are an essential part of our lives. Granted.

But, ask yourself, do you *have* to be online at *all* times? If not, unplug, unhook. That's all. Put your phone down for a fixed time period everyday. Decide your schedule for it: whether it is for two hours every day, or every Sunday. Decide when and for how long you will switch off your gadgets, and then stick to it.

But then, in the time you switch off your phone, also remember to switch off other distractions, and look at your child when you speak to him.

Listen, really listen, don't just sham.

I started by switching off my phone for two hours every day. Two hours in which I would take my daughter to a nearby park, watch her play on the slides and the swing, then get her home and let her soak in a leisurely bath.

This lasted for about six months. In those two hours that I switched off my phone for those six months, nothing catastrophic or disastrous happened. Nothing which needed my immediate attention happened. No emergency, nothing life changing, no matter of life and death left unresolved. Yes, a few conversations were delayed. But that's all.

I realized then that my need to be accessible and online at all times was actually my most ambitious fantasy of holding the world together! That it would fall through the cracks if I was not available for every single minute of the day.

It didn't happen.

What did happen was that I felt lighter, unencumbered and free. Whether it was the absence of the electromagnetic radiation which cellphones emit, or just good old-fashioned fresh air in the park, I can't say. But I started feeling happier and more positive.

That is when I decided to keep my cellphone off for the entire Sunday with even better results.

Watch Your Body Language

This was also a very difficult promise to keep. It was only when I became aware of it that I started making the effort to rectify it.

Just pay attention and observe: How often do we roll our eyes, sigh in exasperation, yell and say insensitive things to our children? Just imagine that your six-year-old has spilled milk all over the kitchen counter which you had painstakingly cleaned a few minutes before. What is your first reaction?

Scene 1: (Yell) Why can't you be careful? You're so clumsy. Now go to your room while I clean up, yet again.

Scene 2: (Exasperated sigh) Oh no! Not again. I'd just finished cleaning up.

Scene 3: Oh! you spilled that by mistake? Do you want to help mama and clean it up?

Which sounds better?

In Scenes 1 and 2, the child is made aware of the fact that he's committed a blunder, and that he should have known better than to increase mama's workload. The unsaid message here is that he is stupid and clumsy, and with your annoyance you are shaming him.

In Scene 3, you are telling your child that you know he spilled milk by mistake. Mistakes happen. Even grown-ups make mistakes, not just children. It doesn't make him a bad boy. But he can help by cleaning it up. The unsaid message here is of patience, acceptance and tolerance.

Now, picture the body language of the little boy after each of the three scenarios just played out.

Scenes 1 and 2 will see him walking away with slumped shoulders, head bent and sad eyes.

Scene 3 will see him walking tall like a little man!

What would you want your little boy to look like?

Screaming in frustration, reprimanding and reproaching is the first instinctive response of adults. But, does it achieve the desired results? Is the message you want to convey which actually reaches the child? Or is there a block in communication here?

The important part here is to keep our body language welcoming and warm, even when we have to explain to the child where he went wrong. Sighs, screams, hands on hips are all aggressive expressions. They may scare your child, but will definitely not help him to acknowledge his mistake and improve his behaviour.

Change the focus from the problem to the solution.

Evaluate the situation in context of its gravity, and respond accordingly.

Once I had turned the microscope inwards and started observing my behaviour, I realized that most often, the magnitude and intensity of *my reaction to my child's mistake depended on my mood, not on her mistake*!

It is human, yes, understandable, yes, but acceptable? No. Our response has to be in proportion to the act committed – stealing from a friend's bag and breaking a vase do not merit the same tone of voice.

But there was another pressing point attached to this, which bothered me even more.

I did not want to be her judge and jury, reading out a verdict and punishing her for every wrongdoing. No, not at all. Just the opposite. I wanted to be her confidante and run-to person. In fact, in times of distress, crisis or wrongdoing, I want to be her refuge and sanctuary, someone she comes running to. Not someone she would feel scared of, or want to run away from.

Remember then, it is important to respond to your child's feelings, not his behavior.

One day, my six-year-old was playing with her friend. She asked me for two *dupattas* which they could each wear as a *saree*. Expertly wrapping the *dupatta* around themselves into *sarees*, and putting them over one shoulder as a *pallu*, they were ready to play Teacher. I could hear them making the dolls sit in a row, giving them homework and then taking turns at becoming teachers. I was smiling to myself as I listened to the two six-year olds teaching the dolls the difference between a 'sleeping line' and a 'standing line'. It was a beautiful scene. They'd been playing animatedly for about an hour, each doll had been severely reprimanded, and the two 'teachers', were giggling happily. When it was time for them to part, I remembered that I had a spare coloured sketch pen set in my cupboard. I took it out, and gave it to my daughter's friend. My daughter snatched it from her hand, and said, "This is mine." Her friend snatched it back, and said, "No, it is mine." Within no time, they were snatching it back and forth and fighting like two kittens. I tried stopping my daughter, explaining, cajoling, and finally screaming at her.

Her friend became quiet, but my daughter started crying. I wanted to punish her then, scream some more at her and show her how angry she'd made me.

But I did none of this. I reminded myself that she was just a six-year-old, feeling hurt that her Mama had given a gift to her friend and not to her, and shouldn't Mama be loving her more than her friend? And also because she'd been the better teacher of the two? And, she wanted a colour sketch pen set too. So what if she already had one.

I picked her up, looked her in the eye, and said softly, "You were such a good teacher that I thought

I'd give you a bigger treat than a sketch pen set you already have. I'm sorry if you felt bad about it."

She immediately smiled. Right through the tears. And asked me, "Really? Is it a surprise? Does it start with 'I'?" Ice cream being her favourite treat, it was not difficult for her to guess.

Shifting the focus had helped me and my daughter to come out of a potentially hazardous situation, unscathed. Without tears, apologies, or hysterical outbursts. Without melodramatic lectures on giving and gratitude, manners and etiquettes!

I had decoded her feelings and responded to them, rather than punishing her for her behaviour. I realized that my new insight into life and living was actually making me a happier person, and a better parent.

The Pressure of Performance

One fine morning in the play school where my daughter studied, the air was buzzing with excitement. Little four-years-old trotted up in fancy costumes to take part in the Annual Day. The previous evening I had been watching my little one whirl in front of the mirror, and I was trying to teach her the right way to do it. "Smile like this, bend like this, hold your arms out a little more, hold your skirt with two fingers…" and so on. But, when I saw her face, my heart went out to her. There was an anxious frown where a smile should have been.

I then realized that I'd been looking at it from the wrong end.

I picked her up, looked into her eyes, and said, "I'm so happy I'll be seeing you on stage. I can't wait." She saw the pride in my eyes, the sincerity in my voice, and her face lit up with the biggest smile I'd ever seen. Her anxious demeanour had made me realize that it was important to take part, not to be perfect.

This realization came to me again as I watched her twirl, "Give me a bell to ring, give me a song to sing..." and found my eyes well with tears. It was not an earth-shattering performance, and my little girl knew it. But she also saw pride in her parents' eyes, she saw that we loved to watch her enjoy what she was doing.

And it has been the same ever since. From that performance to basketball matches, rappelling, river-crossing stints, stage plays, recitals and concerts, it's been a very fulfilling journey. Goof-ups and mistakes aside, there has never been any fear of judgment or criticism. With the pressure of standing first taken off the plate, the sheer joy of performing remained.

Competition and ambition are very important, but they should not take over our lives completely.

In reality shows, little children are pushed beyond their limits, both physically and mentally, their lives robbed of childhood, all to win a competition. It is shameful.

With children today ending their lives because they couldn't score a high percentage in their Board Exams, things have become alarming. *When and how did parents send out the signal that, 'I will love you only if you get 98% or above in your exams?' What made them think that death was better than facing their parents with a lower score?*

Sports, debates, theater and other extra-curricular activities are meant to develop all-round personality, not stunt their growth with comparison and mindless competition. It is the spirit that should be fostered, not the position! Let them enjoy the play and the process, more than the end result. Winning or losing is secondary; it is participating which is important.

When Indian Cricket team is booed and ridiculed after it loses a few matches, it is heart-rending to see the players hiding their faces in front of cameras, taking the backdoor exits to save themselves from the wrath of angry fans and putting on a brave front as their effigies are burnt on their own front lawns! All in the name of love for the game. How much pressure is this love putting on them? Is this the famous sportsman spirit that I want to inculcate in my child? Or can I make the change with my child, right from the first step, by encouraging sincere participation, without the fear of winning or losing? Let's encourage our children to put in their best effort, to give it their all, to put their heart and soul into whatever they do. Then, leave the result to the Almighty.

The return from school is as important as the dropping to school. If possible, make sure the child gets a smiling warm welcome when he comes back from school. Working parents may find it difficult to comply to this one, but it is always possible to leave a little note of affection on the fridge, or taped to their whiteboard. Such messages reassure the children of their parents' love and lessens the loneliness of coming back to an empty house.

Make Time for Fun and Joy

When was the last time you went for a picnic? No, really. A genuine picnic? With packed lunch, bicycles, bats and balls, Frisbees, a board game, a pack of cards maybe. Hot tea in a thermos, an unhurried, unplanned day to just idle in a park. With no agenda. No telephone or any other electronic device. Do you remember just such a day?

The biggest casualty of our well-planned, overcommitted-to-screens life is spontaneity. We can no longer have impulsive, impromptu picnics or playtimes. Everything needs to be planned beforehand, depending on how important these activities are considered in our lives. Being there for your Children.

The most recurrent phrase of our lives is, "We don't have time for that!" There is no time to enjoy, laugh, wonder, observe or just be idle. We think that cramming our day with productive, purposeful and focused activity every single waking minute is the right way to go about our, and our children's lives. *Brahmakumari* philosophy says: "We are human *beings*, not human-*doings*!" There should be time for *'not doing'*. The importance of idleness, of time to get bored, of just being and not doing can never be emphasized enough. The biggest inventions, works of arts and discoveries have happened in these moments of purposeless idleness. If Newton was not idling in the apple orchard, maybe the Law of Gravity, would not have been discovered that day. If Archimedes would not have been enjoying a leisurely tub bath that day, maybe Eureka! would not be a part of our dictionary.

- Go off-script every once in a while. Indulge in the unplanned.
- Encourage impromptu outdoor trips. Be participative and make these fun times. Remember these are deposits in your child's memory bank, and will stay with him forever.
- Permit boredom and idleness. Don't cram your child's day with something or the other to do all the time.
- Inculcate an attitude of celebration in your children – celebrate life, celebrate the blessings of good health and family. There are so many reasons you can think of.

Make evenings and bedtime fun. Make dinners

purely conversation time with the family. If possible, without television, without phones or any other electronic gadgets. Avoid disciplinary actions or rebukes at the dining table, avoid too much attention on the food, and focus more on old-fashioned conversation, with just catching up on each other's day.

Bedtime ritual of tucking-in is as important for the parents as it is for the children. Try to make it as warm and friendly as you can. Ensure that they brush their teeth and change into clean *pyjamas* as a habit, but make allowance for especially tiring days. Then, a few minutes with the child on his bed, and he should feel happy enough to call it a day.

These promises I made to myself are in no way an exaggeration. Nor are they hard to keep. But they do require some groundwork, a little preparation and a lot of efforts to stay on the right track.

How can we do that?

□

Fine Tuning the Parent Mode

Love Yourself

As parents, we forget to take the first step towards being a happy person. *Love Ourselves*.

Do we love ourselves? Or are we always pulling ourselves up for some or the other mistake? Are we not our own harshest critics? How many times do we appreciate ourselves for a job well done? Probably, never. And how many times do we admonish ourselves for our mistakes? Every single time.

How does that make a happy person?

Love spills. There is no way you will love yourself, and not love those around you. If you keep criticizing yourself, you will criticize others also. *Thoughts go from inside to the outside*. If we feel happy inside, it is unlikely that harsh and hurtful words will be spoken, or that the expression will be disapproving, or that the body language will be censorious. A positive frame of mind will not want to make us control, manage or criticize.

Silence your inner critic.

Pursue your interests and hobbies. Don't put your life on hold. I see a lot of parents around me putting off their interests like dancing, music and painting till, 'When the child leaves home for college, and I have all the time in the world!' It doesn't make sense to put off something you enjoy doing. It makes you feel unfulfilled and dissatisfied.

Parenting is not an interim process with a definite time frame.

Parenting requires us to learn the new alphabet, and the new math. For life. Instead of thinking of 1, we now have to think of 4. We have to expand our circle. Think again. Can you involve your children in your hobbies? Is it possible to include them in your music lessons? Can you plan your next white water river rafting in their holidays so that they can also join in? Can you plan your trekking trip when your young ones have scheduled their trip to the grandparents' house?

Prioritize consciously. If you choose to give up your career while your children are young, tell yourself that it's a *choice* you made. *If it feels like a sacrifice, or it makes you feel like a victim, you will never be happy doing it.*

- Invest in yourself. Time, attention, energy and love.
- Take some time out for yourself. Guilt-free, personal, me-time in which you relax and recharge yourself.
- Don't give up on yourself, your hobbies are important. Follow them. This is your life. Don't put it on the back burner.

- Don't criticize yourself too much. Tell yourself you're doing your best, and you will try to do even better.
- Appreciate yourself more often.
- Do what makes you happy. Regularly.
- Take an occasional break without the kids.

Modify Your Perspective

Somewhere along the path of parenting, we lose our perspective. Small things start becoming more important than the bigger picture. We start feeling hassled by small, niggling issues, and forget to see them in the larger context.

That is when small issues become 'problems', minor faults become 'blunders' and a stain on the carpet becomes reason enough for withholding the ice cream treat.

We just need to adjust our vision, and see things through a new pair of glasses.

Let me share six-year-old Myra's mother's experience. She shared this in a Parenting Workshop which I'd attended – "Myra likes making art and craft designs with paper, playing with play-doh, using Scooby strings to make stringy designs. She enjoyed creating with her fingers. But, as a result, there was glue stick, sparkles, coloured dust, crayons, scissors, beads, collage materials, inks, stamp pads, etc. always all over the house. With her two-year-old brother, Naman, always ready to put everything in his mouth, I used to clean up her room, especially her table something like twenty times a day! It was so exhausting, and I used to feel completely drained. One day Myra made a card which read, "I love you, Mommy", complete with glitter, sparkles and little stick-on stars. She gave it to me with a smile, but all I could think was the mess she'd left on the floor of her room, the time it would take me to clean it up and the work I could have done instead. She saw the frown on my face, and her smile faltered. I felt bad, really bad. I wanted to see that smile again. So, I picked her up, gave her a hug, and told her how beautiful the card was. "Really, Mama?" she asked me, "You like it? I thought you were going to get angry with me for making a mess."

The awareness of the mother, and her consequent reaction helped the situation in a little way, but *what kind of a world are we creating if we put a clean table above a child's expression of love?*

It's not as if the mother didn't love her children enough. She did. But her priorities needed to be fine-tuned. Maybe, a creative zone, some drawers and a couple of bins needed to be earmarked inside Myra's room which was out of reach for the little one, and which could be cleaned once a day. *Cleaning is important, and the craft projects are never going to be mess free*. But the problem starts when you make it more important than their creativity and inventiveness.

Remind yourself that neatness is overrated. Again and again. Let them play in the sand, get their hands and clothes dirty, colour outside the lines. If we force them to live with too much method, order and neatness, they will never learn to think outside the box. They will only colour inside the lines all their lives. *The price we pay for obsessive neatness is creativity.* Isn't it a very big price to pay?

Let your child dance to his own tune. Too much conformity breeds mediocrity. Do not fret if he is too different from the other children. Intelligent, original kids are often different, sometimes they are just plain odd. Facilitate and celebrate his difference, encourage him to be out of step, to be unique, to see the world through his own glasses. Why make him 'fit-in', when he can 'stand out?' Ultimately, it's his individuality you will rejoice in, not his 'fitting-in', with the flock.

Encourage boredom. The answer for boredom is not found in structured activities or technological distraction. Free time is the ideal fertile ground in which the child can learn to imagine, invent, explore his inner and outer worlds and create.

We know all this, don't we? But we need to keep reminding ourselves. They may be small points, but they go a long way in keeping us grounded and focused on our task.

With a smile on our lips, and a song in our heart.

For, it is important to enjoy this journey. It will not last very long. Before you know it, they will have flown the nest. So enjoy it today.

□

Strengthen Family Bonds

As parents, we cannot remain in the back seat of our children's lives. We have to be involved, and stay in touch with them. Family ties play an important role in nurturing our relationships, even with our own children. Let's try and forge stronger bonds with them, by paying closer attention to the people in their lives. These are some points which would help.

Develop family rituals. Whether it is visiting relatives every Sunday, putting up lights on every Diwali, weekly grocery shopping, going to a temple once a week, having dinner together every day, whatever works for your family. Make this into a non-negotiable, family-connection time which fosters both routine and closeness in the family. Emergencies aside, make it your own priority, too.

Pay attention to your child's friends and peers. Children are very influenced by their friends, and they play an important role in who they eventually become as an adult. Friends should have a positive influence upon each other. They need to associate with diverse personalities in order to grow. So, a quiet and shy child may need the company of outgoing friends, an overprotected child may need an independent friend.

Rejection, bullying or ridicule by the other kids can lead to permanent dysfunctional behaviour patterns. Similarly, children who find themselves locked in a specific role – for instance, the class entertainer, or the class nerd, or the fat girl – often turn it into a lifelong way of being.

The important thing as a parent is to expose them to different groups – school, sports club group, family and cousins, hobby class group – and provide them ample opportunities to pick up interpersonal skills and learn how to function well in groups with different sets of people. Slowly, you'll watch them getting comfortable and finding like-minded friends to enjoy and grow with.

Draw a line between caring and interference. It is a fine line, sometimes not very clear. Let them handle friend issues to the best of their ability, but intervene if you think it's going out of hand. If his friend's jokes are making him sad, or affecting his self-esteem, step in. Trust your instincts. The damage may not be visible, but permanent, if it is not managed on time.

Encourage family get-togethers with your child's friends. It is a common ground which parents tread, and most of their concerns and fears are shared. Discuss triumphs, grievances, behavioural issues, disagreements, school schedules, or any other topic of concern. Meeting your child's friend's family is a nice way to find out which family does not share our values and way of life, and curb interaction with them.

I had reservations about one of my daughter's friend, whose parents led a bohemian lifestyle. I did not want to pass any judgment on them, but they were very different from our traditional Indian mindset. I didn't want to expose my six-year-old daughter to an alternate world then, when she was young enough not to understand it. I knew it would confuse her at that point in time. However, the lure of the new and the fondness for the friend attracted my daughter. But I was on guard. Her visits to this friend's house were restricted, and I encouraged her to call this friend over at our house instead. I didn't discourage her friendship, I discouraged her to spend time at this friend's house. They soon found alternate arrangements, and starting meeting at other friends' houses, parks and camping trips, and even joined some classes together.

Having friends from diverse backgrounds broadens a child's outlook, but it is not a good idea to be taken unawares by what the friend's family is like.

□

Communication

This is what binds and this is exactly what breaks relationships. Every misunderstanding, conflict and fight boils down to a block in communication.

So it is most important to ease communication with our children, to make it a free flowing two-way channel. For this, we need to start very early on. We have to talk and listen to our children, from childhood, in such a way that our children trust us, and believe that we will understand their point of view.

Accepting/Acknowledging Their Feelings

Don't minimize or diminish their feelings, instead put them in words. You can show them you value them by talking and behaving in a way which affirms their dignity, and sensitively try to see their point of view. They will respect themselves, and others, only when you start by giving them due respect.

When children are experiencing strong emotions, like anger, hurt, sadness or disappointment, it is difficult for them to understand anything. Wait till the storm abates, then bring up the topic again. This time they will listen. And understand.

Choose Words Carefully

Consider the two options here for the same situation:

Scene 1: "Why would you behave so selfish and stupid?"

Scene 2: "Don't keep your ice cream in the cupboard. Your sister has her own share."

Scene 1: "You have become a thief."

Scene 2: "Next time you need money, ask me. Don't take it from my wallet without asking me."

Scene 1: "Don't be selfish."

Scene 2: "Your little brother will feel happy if you share your packet of chips with him."

Scene 1: "Why are you always disorganized?"

Scene 2: "Can I help you to clean your study table?"

Scene 1: "Why are you never punctual?"

Scene 2: "Please call me if you are going to be late."

Scene 1: "Why can't you stop asking questions?"

Scene 2: "I like it that you are so curious."

Scene 1: "I've done so much for you. You are so ungrateful."

Scene 2: "Let us be grateful for what we have. I'll get you a better phone when I think you need it."

Scene 1: "I won't let you go for the party if you don't clean up your filthy room."

Scene 2: "Do you want me to help you, clean up your room before you go for the party?"

Empathy and compassion should be the cornerstones of communication with children. Communicate to heal, not wound. Words should be like flowers, not pins.

Blaming, accusing, using harsh words, threatening, giving orders, comparing, being sarcastic, playing martyr, prophesying doom are toxic parental habits and erode the child's confidence.

Avoid Negative Labels

Labelling is Disabling

Negative image shown by parents and parental figures distorts self-image of the child. You want your child to improve and become better, but giving him a negative label will only make him feel trapped inside the negative image you've given him. Locking him in a negative role will burden him for the rest of his life. Counselling sessions reveal that childhood tags provided by family and friends are the toughest to shake off and outgrow. *Negative emotions work like bullets.* They corrode, and obstruct behavioural changes and growth. Instead, use positive words to boost self-esteem in your child. **Show them a new picture of themselves.** If your child has been called 'irresponsible' in school by a teacher, praise him for being 'responsible' when he looks out for his younger sibling in the park. **Put them in situations where an alternate side can be explored.** And then remember to praise them for it. Also, let them overhear you say something positive about them. It will boost self-confidence and encourage positive behavioural traits.

Stereotyping and typecasting are major pitfalls. Let us not do it with our children. Like, *boys* don't cry and *girls* play with dolls. In India, there is a very distinct difference between the way a son and a daughter are brought up. There is an effort to make a man out of a little boy, even as he is struggling to learn how to walk! He is expected to hide his fears and hurts, he is told that playing with dolls and kitchen sets is a girly thing to do, and he is expected to enjoy the rough and tumble activities. After all, it is the masculine thing to do. How can he not learn how to be a man right at his mother's knee?

And, a girl is flooded with the colour pink, frills and laces, hair accessories and dolls. Even if she says she doesn't like any of it. How can she not? She just isn't feminine.

Let us not do this.

Listen attentively to them. Listening to our children is a bigger art than talking to them. What is your reaction when your child tells you about, for instance, his fight with a friend? Do you hear him out, or just scold him, or explain to him how wrong it is?

Next time you are tempted to spew forth your wisdom, desist! Listen. Really listen. Let go of what you are doing, look at him and listen. Give brief statements that let your child know that you are truly listening:

- Could you repeat that?
- Where were you standing when this happened?
- It must have bothered you.
- Why do you think he behaved the way he did?
- Did the teacher understand your point of view?
- I can understand it must have made you angry.
- It was not a good day for you.

Do not start with a critical or sarcastic comment, like:

- What trouble did you get in today?
- Why have you made such a long face?
- Oh no, not the sad face again!

The message here is that the child's feelings are important, they are not to be trivialized. That getting angry is understandable, but fist-fight and abuses are not. That the child can come with any problem to the parent without fear of being admonished, ignored or judged. That you are there to heal his emotional wounds.

It will reinforce a lifelong pattern in their behaviour; they will never ignore or trivialize their own feelings or the feelings of their loved ones.

Ignoring emotions doesn't work. Because, like rivers, you cannot stop them, but you can direct their course. They have to be acknowledged and dealt with.

An important aspect here, though, is another thought: Why don't children want to share their mistakes with parents? Is it because *parents do not share their mistakes with their children*? Do the children think that parents consider admitting mistakes a flaw in the personality? It is up to us to show them that we are a sum total of all our mistakes, that *we bear our scars with pride because they have made us who we are, that our personality and attitudes are a cumulative of every blunder and slip-up we ever made*. There is no shame in making mistakes; we all do. Swapping stories is a nice way to bond and learn. It can become a fun family ritual. And a great way of seeking solutions.

Encourage Honesty with Your Child

This has to be a two-way process. Never lie to your child, and encourage him never to lie to you. We parents tend to lose our cool when we know our child is lying, especially when the lie is obvious. Like a child insisting that he didn't eat the ice cream when he has ice cream smudged all over his clothes. What is the most common parental reaction here?

"Stop lying. I know it was you."

Child, scared and defensive, "No, it wasn't me. I did not eat the ice cream."

Now the basic ground rule of expecting honesty is to *not* ask the questions to which we already know the answer, especially those which may make the child resort to defensive lying. Don't corner him right there and then. Let it pass. For the time. Else, it will become a habit and he will tell lies whenever he is pushed into a corner.

The desire for mutual honesty also demands that we be prepared for some bitter truths. It will not always be easy, or pleasant. And, *our reactions will decide whether honesty will become the best policy for them the rest of their lives or not.* When six-year-old Sara told her mother that she hated her grandmother, her mother reacted strongly with, "Oh! no, you don't. That is such a nasty thing to say." Instead of asking why she hated her grandmother, the mother became angry. "You never say such a thing again, or you're going to be grounded," threatened her mother. "Now tell me, do you hate your grandmother?" "No, mom," said the little girl, thinking to herself that it was not wise to tell the truth. That a little lie was a better way to handle sticky situations. Maybe if the mother had asked her the right question, Sara would have told her that she hated her grandmother because she had knitted a sweater for her younger brother, but not for her. Things could have been resolved, and Sara could have had the courage to tell her mother a bigger, but more bitter, truth the next time.

Sometimes a lie may not be a lie, it may just be an active imagination or an expression of a desire. A small boy saying 'I got a real airplane on my birthday,' cannot be termed a *liar*. The important thing is to distinguish between a fantasy and a lie, between wishful thinking and plain dishonesty. *Lies tell truths about what the speaker wants.* This child could be signalling his desire to travel in an airplane, maybe to visit a grandmother he is missing.

Communication is a two-way process, and a parent's response or reaction will determine the flow of this communication. Censure and disapproval will stem the flow, and mutual respect will encourage open communication.

As a parent, we have to guard against falling into the pattern of some **Common Adult reactions**—

Philosophical – "There will always be someone who doesn't like you."

Threats – "If you don't switch off the TV right now, you can forget about going to the party."

Bribe – "If you give your brother the TV remote, I'll give you an extra scoop of ice cream."

Defend the other side – "He didn't mean to hurt you when he pushed you."

Denial of feelings – "Of course, you don't want your brother dead."

Advice – "If your friend is fighting with you, you must tell the teacher."

Accusation – "You create trouble wherever you go."

Insults and Criticism – "You are such a disgrace to my name."

Pity – "Oh, you poor boy! I feel so bad that you fell down in school today."

Psychoanalysis – "You did not want to see what is inside that toy which you just broke. You need to prove that you are strong."

These reactions don't add anything to the solution being sought by your child. It is easier for adults to fall into these patterns, and respond with any one of the oft-repeated appeaser, but ask yourself, will it really help the situation in hand? Or is the child looking for some other answers? Avoid hurtful and sarcastic comments. Parental criticism just creates more resentment in the child. It will only teach him to see the worst in people around, and condemn and criticize them at all times.

Problem Solving

It is important to understand how to raise children and teens to be emotionally and socially intelligent, so they will be able to handle both good and adverse times. For that, do not be ready to dole out how-to's at every possible step. When you sense your child needs guidance or solution to a problem, do not offer it instantly. Instead, pause. Then ask him, "Hmm...how are you thinking of handling this?"

Familiarize yourself with what is on your child's mind. It may seem trivial to you, but it is important for him. Your experience and insight may give him a quick fix solution, but it will also slowly become the crutch he'll start using instead of his own feet. Do not give him that crutch.

So, first, **hear them out**. Ask them how they would like to deal with the situation. Brainstorm with them. Assess their suggestions, and point out the merits and demerits of the different courses of action. Work out a plan with them involved.

Consider this Situation :

Your fifteen-year-old son comes back after a school game, and complains that the referee was unfair. That he should have been granted the goal, and that their team's win depended on that goal. And that he's going to complain to the headmaster about it.

What is your first instinct? To tell him 'it's just a school game', 'the referee must have right', 'there's always a next game where you can excel'. Or some such platitude. To calm him down. But, will it sort out what's weighing on his mind?

Instead, ask him to sit down. Then, ask him about the game. 'When did the game start?', 'Which team was leading till half time?', 'Who scored the goal?', 'What was the referee's reason for not giving you the goal?', and 'Why do you think he was unfair?', 'How did that make you feel?' 'What do you want to do about it?'

Take him through the problem-solving process. Get him to relate the entire sequence. Factor in the possibility that he could have been mistaken. Very subtly. Allow him to soak it in. Get him to see the situation with fresh eyes. Then suggest options, and ask him what he would like to do.

Lead him to arrive at the solution himself. Don't provide it to him.

If he is willing to let it go, he's learnt that there will be a next time, and he may have been mistaken in thinking that the referee was biased.

If he's not willing to let it go, he's learnt to stand up for himself when he is wronged.

In either case, he can rely on you giving him a patient ear for his problems. And he knows he can come back for your guidance and counsel whenever the need arises.

Discipline

"Where did we ever get the crazy idea that in order to make children do better, first we have to make them feel worse? Think of the last time you felt humiliated or treated unfairly. Did you feel like cooperating or doing better?" – Jane Nelsen.

Parents often confuse discipline with punishments, reprimands, penalties, withdrawal of benefits, timeouts and forfeits. Spare the rod and spoil the child was the norm of many generations, and was adhered to as strictly as a religious tenet. But, does it work like that? If modifying behaviour is our aim, then will spanking the child get the desired result?

Positive Discipline

"Everyday injustices, harsh words, bullying, humiliation, callousness and the misguided sense that children are dumb and don't really understand much takes its toll on all of us. We insist that children must be moulded and trained and fundamentally changed from their natural state of being a child. It is a universal assumption that innocence is the antithesis of smartness." – Natasha Badhwar, blogger, columnist and mother.

Parents need to set limits, that's true. But they need to set those limits with compassion, empathy and understanding. Aggression and punishments only reinforce the belief that hostility and violent behaviour is acceptable. Punishing will make kids angry, wary and defensive. They will try to defend themselves, and explain why they did what they're being pulled up for. In the process, they may even tell lies or half-truths, create melodrama, throw tantrums, resort to infantile distraction tactics, and emotional drive like, "You don't love me!" Anything to escape punishment and the accompanying feelings of low self-worth. But, will they change the undesired behaviour?

Our sole objective, as parents, should not be to reform and teach them a lesson. They aren't merely objects to be moulded. Children learn what they see their parents and role models doing. This puts the responsibility of children's behaviour, to a large extent, on the parents' shoulders. Parents have to treat them the way they want them to treat others: with kindness, consideration and forgiveness.

That doesn't mean we don't lay down some basic ground rules – like no lying, no stealing, no hitting, no hurting and a whole lot of more don'ts as they keep growing up. But these lessons have to be internalized and accepted as part of the child's value system. Which means that even if no adult is watching, and there is no fear of punishment, a certain code of conduct is still followed. Children should *want* to do what's right. They have to learn to take responsibility for their own actions and behaviour. How does that come about?

What can be the roadmap to guiding the course of our child's life in the positive direction? How can we evoke in them the desire to be their best selves?

The first step, as parents, is to learn to manage our own attitude and emotions. Re-work your own persona in such a way that your negative and destructive habits do not ruin your child's personality.

Indian mothers tend to go heavy on the **self-sacrificing** role – 'I gave up my career to be a Stay-at-Home Mother.' 'I did not go for a movie since it was my child's tuition time.' 'I don't socialize on week nights because it disrupts my child's schedule.'

Fine. Nice thinking. But, ask yourself, 'Is this mindset making me feel more like a helpless victim?, because, if I'm not happy doing what I am doing, then I will keep bringing it up and expecting my family to compensate for my sacrifice. *A better idea is to accept the parameters I have to work within to do what's best for my family, and to make it a choice, not a sacrifice.* Then, work towards self-development within the said parameters. Pick up skills, learn crafts and focus on growing as a person. Ask yourself: Can I use this career stopgap time to learn driving? Or painting? Or any one of the thousands of skills and arts which make us grow as a person.

Another attitude which children learn from us is **anger management**. It is natural to get angry. Getting angry is not wrong, it is how we express anger that is right or wrong. We have to accept that it is not possible to expect that you, or your child, will never get angry. In fact, in certain situations, absence of anger could even be seen as indifference by the child.

So, how does one define acceptable anger? *Emotional health and well-being depends on the correct expression of our feelings.* There is no reason to hide them, or suppress them. Hysterical reactions, violent outbursts and belligerent words will only show our children that all this is an acceptable vent. Shouting and screaming at them and asking *them* to speak politely is a wasted effort. **You cannot expect them to do what you *say*, they will do what you *do*.** Restraint is the key here. If you act out when you are upset, your daughter will do the same. If you take a deep breath and become composed before you address a potentially turbulent situation, she will do exactly the same.

I remember a day when I had gone to a friend's house whose mother-in-law had been ailing for a long time. She'd had a particularly rough day, with the maid not turning up and the baby throwing up all day. Her twelve-year-old son walked in from school just then, threw his books on the bed and started complaining about his teacher, "She is so mean, she punished me for no fault of mine. All my friends were talking, but she singled me out."

My friend lost her cool then, and screamed at him, "You are a selfish child. Can't you see I've had a rough day? Can't you at least shut up about your troubles for once?" And so on.

He looked hurt, then stormed up to his room and locked himself in. My friend felt worse than she'd been feeling already.

I could see that both of them were not wrong in their place. They were both angry. But their anger needed a more acceptable vent. And, not on each other.

When children are angry, all they want is the reassurance of parental love. Not lectures. Not angry, hurtful words. Definitely not punishment. When you're angry, don't try to punish your child and teach him "a lesson." It definitely will not be the lesson you want him to learn. Instead just stop. Take a deep breath. Walk away. Even if you're in the middle of a sentence. You're not losing face here, you're teaching responsible anger management. Wait till you and your child are calm before bringing it up again.

They don't *know* you've had a rough day, and they have rough days of their own. Would we want them mirroring us on our rough days?

Behaviour and personality building is a complex process, and there are many variables at play here. But there's one basic rule – what goes in, comes out.

Taking an example from the manufacturing process of products –

Input → Process → Output

If the input is of good quality, the product will be of superior quality. But, if the input is faulty or defective, the output is bound to be substandard.

In parenting situations, input is the different factors which combine to create the child's personality. And output is the child's behaviour. Changes have to be made at the input stage if any behavioural modification is sought.

The next step is to show unconditional love, empathy and support. At all times, especially during the times the child has done something wrong. In the heat of the moment, it is not possible to teach or learn; it is more important to calm the child down. Let him take time to deal with his anger, defensiveness and embarrassment as best as he can. Be around. Show with your body language that you are not judging him, just guiding him to do the right thing. That you love him NO MATTER WHAT. That his behaviour is unwanted, but he is not. That your love for him is not so fragile that his wrongdoing can change it. It is important.

Maintain emotional connect. Connection is important at all times. And it is a very integral part of the process of discipline. When kids feel disconnected because of emotional or physical distance from us, they will not be open to our influence. But, once that distance is repaired, they will want to behave well and listen to us. The secret is to not talk down to them, or punish them in the name of discipline, but to address them as adults who have their own moods and fears.

Reinforce good behaviour. Whether it is looking after siblings, saying Please and Thank You, feeding the pet, being punctual for her classes, doing homework, being polite with the family and other desirable etiquettes and life skills you want her to imbibe. Acknowledge, appreciate, applaud. Reward for positive behaviour works better than punishment for the negative behaviour.

Choose your words and the tone carefully. And your body language should be in sync with your words. Sincerity is more important than we realize. Children catch our vibes before they hear our words, so do not make the mistake of saying one thing and meaning another. Talk as respectfully as would talk to an adult friend. Discipline does not need a harsh tone of voice, or cruel words to be effective. At all times, but especially when the child is misbehaving, respond rather than react.

Consider this situation now:

Nine-year-old Amardeep is throwing a tantrum for a new toy, and after the mother explains that she cannot take him to the market right away, he tears his sister's copy in anger.

Scene I: Mother screams and yells at Amardeep, threatens dire consequences and tells him that she will not get him that toy, or any other toy, no matter what. More screams and tears follow.

Scene 2: Mother sits down next to him, looks into his eyes and says in a controlled voice, "You are furious, I can see that. So am I. Let's talk when we are both not angry. No more tears, no more tantrum."

Scene 3: Mother says, "You will apologize to your sister right away. I will not listen to you till you have done that."

Now, let's turn the spotlight on the boy and see how he feels after each of these scenes.

In scene 1, the boy feels angry and unloved, with the added *helplessness and hopelessness of not being understood by his mother and there's the feeling of guilt since he knows he has done something wrong*. The cocktail of these feelings will not let him see his mistake and change undesirable behaviour.

In scene 2, the boy knows he has done something wrong, but feels that his mother loves him and is willing to understand his point of view, she talks to him like he is a responsible adult and that is precisely how he will behave when he calms down. *The mother's calm tells him that anger and disappointment can be expressed in a more non-destructive way, which is the right mode of behaviour.* Above all, he is assured that mother will not stop loving him. The stimulus for the right reaction and correction of behaviour is provided very beautifully.

In scene 3, the boy feels that the mother loves only the sister, because her only concern is the sister's feelings and not his. He feels guilty, insecure and unworthy of the mother's love. And angrier than before. Now, will he change his undesirable behaviour? **Are you, as a parent, building him up, or tearing him down?** Ask yourself.

Set rules and limits empathetically, and explain why they are important. Saying only 'Because I say so', is a dead end, and will not elucidate the importance of the said rules. Acknowledge the child's viewpoint, but clarify why it is still important to adhere to them. Be willing to listen and understand their perspective.

"I know you would like to go for a sleepover at your friend's house, but in our house, we don't do that."

"I know you'd like me to extend your curfew time for the party, but at your age, 11 pm is a reasonable hour."

"I know you are scared about telling me that you drove my car without any adult supervision, but I want to know the truth."

"I know you were angry when you abused your sister, but I want you to remember that in our house, we choose our words more carefully when we are furious."

Spell out the rules clearly. Repeatedly. Reinforce them with your own behaviour.

Reinforce the importance of mending. Again, with example, compassion and empathy. Teach kids to clean up and repair as much as they can. The easy availability of staffers makes it easy for them to avoid cleaning up after spilling or breaking. But enforce it by doing it yourself. Lead by example. **My mess, my responsibility.** It is a starting point for a desirable behavioural characteristic, and will carry forward to mending and cleaning up in relationships also. *Words of apology and hugs will become the paper towels needed to clean up the mess,* but it has to start with the acknowledging of responsibility.

Inculcate religious tolerance. This is a very important, but highly neglected, part of the parenting process in most Indian households. It is vital to introduce your children to other religions and expose them to their religious rituals and practices. Make sure you have friends of diverse ethnicity and religions and take them to temples, mosques, gurudwaras and churches. Enforce that the *Gayatri Mantra is as important to know as 'Our father, who art in heaven....'* Discuss highlights of different religious texts with your teenagers and encourage them to read on their own. It not only broadens our horizons, it also makes us more accepting and understanding.

In the current Indian scenario where religion is used by politicians as a trump card to create strife, it has become more important than ever before. Secular and peaceful mutual co-existence, respect for other religions and liberty to pursue one's faith are the cornerstones of a civilized society. And they start right at home.

Listen to the unsaid words. Forge a strong connect with your children, be clued-in to them, such that you know what they mean even when they cannot articulate or express it. *Connect before you start to correct.* His misconduct and tantrum is an expression, however wrong you may think, of a valid and important need. Think about what he is unable to express – is he tired, or sleepy, or just seeking your attention? Recognize that need and address it. **Express, share, vent, listen, be fully present, give big hugs.** Listen carefully to what they say, without judging, without lecturing and without moralizing.

An important thing to remember here is that *not everything, every act needs to be corrected. Parents tend to fuss over non-essentials a great deal.* And overthink. Is it really such a big deal if your seven-year-old wants to watch cartoons? See the larger picture here. After two years, he will not *want* to watch cartoons even if you ask him to. Give them space, and acknowledge that he is a person, with his own wishes, moods, hopes and attitude.

Encourage discussion with your children where they get to say what's on their minds without being rebuked or preached. Value honesty above right and wrong. Let them understand the consequences of their actions, let them know that you are their go-to person at all times. No discussion is taboo, no conversation is off-limits, and no thought too small to be shared. Let them share their feelings. And remember not to judge them for their feelings. Explain that they do not have to be ashamed or embarrassed to talk about any feeling they may have. It is important for them to know what they are feeling, to articulate and express their feelings if they are to learn how to deal with them.

Manage Television Viewing

It's an undeniable part of our lives. The main downside to unrestricted television viewing is that it encourages violence, glorifies anti-social behaviour, and trivializes socially acceptable behaviour. Sex and brutality are a part of most programs being aired today. A good idea is to fix certain times and programs in which the children will watch television.

With these basic ground rules, discipline should not be difficult to ensure. And again, remind yourself, that your parental instinct overrides any rules, at any time. The same situation may merit different treatment with different children, or even with the same child at different times. Go by your gut.

□

Safety Rules

This is the biggest concern and fear factor of parents' lives today. With crime rate escalating, accidents happening right outside our doorstep and Internet inviting strangers right into our bedrooms, keeping our family safe and threat-free has become a big challenge.

Safety means guarding the health, well-being and lives of our children.

Satellite television has exposed our children to the Western culture, and the definition of taboo has changed dramatically. Young impressionable minds see kissing and lovemaking scenes on television and they open up porn sites while searching for something perfectly innocent. The concept of, 'fit for family viewing', has become very flexible in the last 15 years. So, how does one protect their innocence? Exposure comes before maturity and understanding, before the child is old enough to know what's going on. Where does it start?

With you. The Parent. Keep your antennae tuned to their wavelength, in such a way that any untoward change sets off alarm bells in your mind. Stay connected to them. At all times.

Most evenings, I see small children in strollers, accompanied by their *ayahs* and servants. In parks, the *ayahs* are huddled together exchanging gossip, or flirting with servants, while the baby in the pram cries, unattended. At times, I see the *ayah* eating ice cream, and feeding the baby from the same cup with the same spoon! Infants take a lot of our energy, and at one level, I can understand the mother's need for some breathing time while baby is outdoors, enjoying fresh air and new sights. Children enjoy being outside. But at what cost?

Children need most attention in the first three years of their life when they cannot express. Then, we can slowly start relaxing it since they can tell us, if not very clearly, then at least by behavioural cues. If baby has to be let out in the pram in the evenings, and a family member is unavailable at that time, it is best that he is around the house where the mother can keep an eye on him. Very reliable and loving servants also can't be trusted completely to feed the child, since their level and understanding of hygiene is not the same as ours.

Nanny cams are a useful tool to keep an eye. Recently, in Delhi, there was the horrific case where the *ayah* was dressing the infant in rags and handing him over to beggars at the red light intersection in exchange for a sum of money while the parents were at work. Such situations are any parent's nightmare!

When children start communicating and expressing themselves, there are a few rules we should keep in mind to ensure their safety at all times.

Open communication channels between parents and children is the first and foremost prerequisite to keeping them safe. **Every risk, abuse or threat that we can think of, from drugs, underage driving, drinking, sexual predators, and breaking the law, can be dealt with by building a trusting relationship with the children.** Encourage them to share what's on their mind. Do not shrug off distinct changes in behaviour as a part of growing up. Make your children your highest priority. *Be their refuge and sanctuary so they come to you during the times of distress.*

Sharpen their reflexes by articulating difficult situations and appropriate responses. Outline situations and ask them what their behaviour would be if that situation presented itself. What would you do if the friend's brother asked you to take a sniff from his stash of drugs? What would you do if the friend took out his father's gun to show you how it's loaded? What would you do if the servant wanted to show you something in his room when no one was at home? What would you do if your thirteen-year-old friend took out his father's car without telling anyone and promised to take you for a ride? What would you do if your friend tried to show you porn? Teach them the importance of leaving the room without any explanation if their gut says something's wrong. *Leave first. Explain later.*

Get to know the families before you send your child to someone's house. And be alert about your child's reaction after he comes back. Is he distant? Defiant? Quiet?

Talk to him about what goes on at his friends' houses. Make it your business to know. *After all, your child's life depends on it.* Ask questions like: Are the kids with any adult family member, or only with servants? Is there someone to ensure that they're not taking out their bicycles in the middle of the afternoon to race up and down the roads? Does their computer have a child safety password protection? Is liquor kept under lock and key? Do they own and display firearms? Is the gas plate in the kitchen accessible to the children? And knives? Is there any pet in the house which is violent, or not vaccinated?

Intervene if your child is affected by ragging or bullying in school and college. Empower your children by building their confidence and self-esteem. Need for acceptance, vulnerability, pressure to fit-in are some of the reasons why children put up with misbehaviour and bullying at school. Saying things like 'Man up and face them,' are a futile exercise and will only make them feel more inadequate. Help them to forge healthy friendships, peer relationships and inculcate social interpersonal skills. Comfort and reassure them, and step in if your child does not want to go to school or is withdrawn and depressed.

There have been cases of students committing suicides in colleges after being harassed in the name of ragging. Don't wait for authorities to intervene, initiate them if you see the telltale signs of pressure on your child. Change the school or college if necessary. **Saving life is more important than saving face.**

Educate your child about 'appropriate' and 'inappropriate' touching. Body education has to start right at the beginning. Explain that no one has the right to touch, caress, fondle or hug the child if they don't want it. **Respect their voice.** No saying "Come on, don't be a fuss pot. Uncle only wants to give you a peck!" No forcing them for a hug or kiss if they don't want it. **Listen to their No! so they realize that their No! matters.** As a parent also, do not hug or kiss your children when they do not want contact. **Respect their boundary.** Teach your child that his body is private, and no one – no family, no friends, no siblings, no coach, no tutor – can touch it against his wish. Put it into words, don't shy away from explaining and asking questions. Tell them it's alright for the child to run away, scream or shout for help if someone is making him uncomfortable.

Molestation is an ever present menace, both for girls and boys, and leaves permanent scars. Keeping your child safe from sexual abuse, with you identifying the support system of cousins, friends and other family members who can be allowed to be with your children alone. Statistics show that most molesters are well-known, well-loved and well-trusted friends, family members and teachers. **Respect your child's opinion.** If he says he doesn't like a cousin or a friend's mother, don't preach, question or defend. Just listen, and file away for future reference. What is important is that he doesn't like someone, not *why* he doesn't like that particular person.

Role-play difficult situations and appropriate responses. What if someone gives you a chocolate and asks you to come with them? What would you do if a car stops near you and a smiling woman asks you for directions? And then asks you to take her there? What would you do if someone threatens you at gunpoint to come with them without telling anyone?

As a parent, our duty is to teach them that it is most important to trust yourself. **Staying safe is more important than being polite.** Not every adult means well, not every adult has to be obeyed.

Drive Safe, Drive Well. In our hasty, rushed lives when our only focus is on getting from Point A to Point B, we sometimes overlook the most basic safety guidelines. Some drills have to become a part of our routine. Like, check that your car is centrally locked, seat belts are fastened, children are strapped in their car seats, ask the child to step out of the car only after making sure there are no rushing cars whizzing past his side, and, above all, make sure you don't leave a sleeping baby inside the car. Yes. You'll be surprised how often that happens. Follow traffic rules religiously so that they become ingrained in your children. Do not make calls, or text, while driving. No matter how urgent. Most accidents happen like this, and most behaviours are picked up childhood onwards by watching parents.

When children start driving, make sure that they drive safe, and keep yourself informed about their late night whereabouts. Make it a habit for them to call you and inform when they reach, *and* when they leave. No matter how late the hour. Drinking and driving, or being driven by a drunk or an inexperienced driver are an absolute no-no. Enforce this strongly. Again and again. Tell them you will come and pick them any time they're uncomfortable about the driver, or their own driving. Repeat stories about car accidents involving rash and reckless driving. Highlight the loss and devastation the family has to live through after losing a family member.

Safety in public, and in public transport has to be taught. Start by developing the habit of being aware and alert when the children start stepping outside the house. Crossing the road in the right way has to be reinforced every time. *Ask them to pay attention to the world around them,* which means no talking on the cellphone, no texting, no listening to music with earphones and no being lost in your own world. Look around. Is someone staring at you? Stalking you? Creeping you out? Someone dubious who's there every morning you board your bus? Or who bumps into you every time you leave for your coaching? *Change schedules, change routes, report. Do not ignore.* If it still persists, seek help immediately.

When children are young teens, they will start using public transport. Initiate them into using buses, autos and the metros. Start by letting him travel in a friends' group, but prepare him mentally too. Ask him questions like: What will you do if you realize that your wallet is stolen? What happens if you and your friend get separated while boarding the metro? What if your bag falls on the metro tracks, or in the middle of the road while you are crossing it? Make sure their phones have emergency safety apps, which alert you promptly in case of a need.

Safety in parties is another set of rules which has to be instilled in the children. Once the young teens start going out for parties, unattended, a few rules help them stay safe. There has to be a minimum age limit for drinks, and has to be enforced rigidly. A curfew limit for returning home is essential, but a little flexibility is desirable. *Be a parent, not a drill sergeant*. Enforce that your young adult does not accept drinks (water or soft drinks included), from anyone in the party, but goes to the counter where water or drinks are being served. The date rape drugs (the three most common and easily available ones are Rohypnol, GHB, Ketamine), are a looming menace in today's world, and vigilance is the only way to stay safe. Being driven home by friends who've been drinking is an absolute no, either make sure they have a reliable driver, or go yourself to pick and drop your children from parties. There can be no compromises here.

Keep your communication channels open. Ask uncomfortable questions. Talk constantly. Listen more. When it comes to parenting, over communication is always better. It will help you stay connected, and make your child feel safe. Help them to develop sound judgment, social intelligence and improve their reflexes. Teach them to rely more on their instincts. Ensure that they are not gullible and vulnerable. After all, their lives, and yours too, depends on it.

Online safety is a big challenge. This has to start with the parents. Try to keep the computer in a high-traffic area of your home. Next, install child safety software on the computer. These act as filters and monitoring tools, and effectively block out many inappropriate sites. Most porn sites have names quite close to the gaming sites which children surf. The first option that appears on the screen after typing a kiddie game is most likely to be a porn site. The software takes care not to let such sites open. But it is not 100 percent foolproof. It is important to be vigilant. Very young children need adult supervision for computer time.

With older children, spell out certain rules clearly. And reinforce them regularly. For example:

- No giving out of any personal information without informing the parents. No sharing online of home address, parents' phone number, parents work schedule, tuition timings, class schedules, or holiday plans.
- Passwords, ATM pins should not be shared. Even with best friends. After using a public computer, make sure that the account is logged out before leaving the terminal.

- Screen names should not have any personal information, like date of birth or home address.
- Don't post photos or videos without informing the parents.
- Don't respond to online ads, or buy/sell stuff online without informing the parents.
- Do not agree to meet anyone you've met online, or on some social site. People online may not be who they say they are. A "10-year old girl from Delhi", may well be a middle-aged pervert from Patiala!
- Report online stalking, suggestive, filthy, obscene and uncomfortable chats.
- Talking about sexual topics online with strangers is not cool. It may lead to unwanted sexual solicitation. Sexting, taking and sharing nude or sexually provocative pictures or videos is an absolute No. Online predators lurk at every corner.
- How you behave online is a reflection of you. Be polite, respectful. Do not post angry, aggressive or hurtful comments. Don't be a cyberbully, and don't put up with one.
- Download files from secure networks only. Malicious software cannot only put your privacy or financial data at risk, it can also trick you into giving out important information, like ATM pin, credit card password and online banking password.
- Guard against identity theft. This is done

when enough information is collected online to impersonate the child and create an identity to post mean, objectionable or even illegal content in your child's name.

- Be careful about the apps your child is using on her mobile, since some apps track your child's location, while some ask for permission to access all kinds of information. Read the fine print carefully, and then advise them whether that app should be downloaded or not.

Shyness or an introvert nature is not a disease to be cured.

Neither is shyness an issue which needs to be addressed and fixed. Some children like to be by themselves, and they like to be quiet around people they are not comfortable with. It is fine. Let them be. Do not think they will grow up to be antisocial lonely adults with no friends. Do not force them to talk, or push them into conversations.

We see parents around us treating their children like battery operated toys, asking them to spout nursery rhymes or perform some mimicry, or even recite part of some morning assembly speech! Children who don't like performing at their parents' behest are often held up for ridicule. It is important to remember that our children are human beings; they are mini adults. They have complete right to refuse to do it, they have the right to retreat to their rooms if they are not feeling social enough to interact with your friends, or even their own.

Handling Exam Stress

A spate of student suicides in the years 2005-10 following poor Board Exam results, set alarm bells ringing in the minds of parents and educators alike. A Suicide Helpline was set up for Board students, and Kapil Sibal, the HRD Minister, had made Board Exams optional for all Central Board of Secondary Education (CBSE) class X students in 2011 to reduce stress levels as part of an education system overhaul.

But children have to give exams. That's a fact of life. How can we empower them enough to handle the pressure of exams without crumbling? This is our biggest challenge as parents.

Why have school exams become a matter of life and death? Why is there so much competition in our minds? Why is coming first or winning the medal the only important thing here? When I hear children talking among themselves it mostly goes like: "If I don't get such-and-such grade, my parents will kill me." "If I don't stand first, I'd much rather die than face my parents." "If I don't win the medal, I'd rather kill myself than go home."

Why do children talk like this? What can we do to change this mindset?

First of all, take a deep breath and de-stress yourself. It is your energy and vibrations which your child is going to absorb. Rethink your own priorities, adjust your own looking glass. Believe it when you tell your child that you will not be disappointed if he doesn't come first, so long as he worked hard. What is important is his sincere preparation for the exams, not the report card.

Emphasize the importance of hard work and preparation.

Well begun is half done. Truly. Help them plan their timetable and study schedule. Sit down with them and ask them to focus on which subjects need more attention than others. Plan tuitions, study group options or seek help from teachers. Be proactive. The important thing is to put in sincere hard work. Teach your children the importance of putting their weight behind diligent study schedules *right through the year*. Being scared in the last few days before exams will only put undue pressure.

Trust Children

If you want your child to take examinations with confidence, start trusting your child more. If he says he doesn't need tuition for Physics, don't push him. Don't impose your own knowledge on him. If he says he performs better in a group study situation, believe him. Don't question.

Trust him to know his own strength and weakness. And do not judge this by the grades he get. Never, never say 'I told you so', if he doesn't fare well. Trust doesn't mean he gives you the desired result. It just means you have confidence in him to be able to take decisions for himself.

Make time for a few moments of meditation. It helps in calming their minds and aiding focus. Sit down in a quiet corner, close your eyes and take long, deep breaths for a few minutes. Start when they are young, so it becomes a part of the daily schedule.

Don't make a big deal of low grades. And do not compare grades. Absolutely not. Never ask, 'What did your friend get?' 'How come she got more when you have the same tutor?' Don't turn friends and peers into competitors, enforce that the only competition your child has is with himself. He has to be better than he was. By working hard. That's all. Never tease or ridicule a child for his grades, never belittle or insult him.

Numbers should not dictate the worth of a person. Whether they are on a report card, or in his bank.

Inculcating the Right Values

> "These are hard times for children, and so for parents. There has been a sea change in the nature of childhood over the last decade or two, one that makes it harder for children to learn the basic lessons of the human heart and one that ups the ante for parents who used to pass these lessons on to the children they love. Parents have to be smarter about teaching their children basic emotional and social lessons."
>
> **—Daniel Goleman**

We all want to raise children with the right kind

of values, children who are responsible, considerate, cooperative and upright. But how do we start?

Again, the answer is simple—it starts at home. More importantly, it starts with YOU!

Reinforce the importance of family. In India, the family system is slowly shifting and changing. It is important to explain the sanctity of family as a unit to our children. The fabric of our society, and hence our civilization, depends on it. Family is a lifelong commitment, an emotional investment with a no-return policy. *There is no choice but to have mutual respect and goodwill with family members, because family comes with a lifetime guarantee, no-cancellation option and no expiry date.* There will be problems, conflicts and disagreements. Granted. But, they have to be sorted out. This is the bottomline.

Guide, be a suitable role model and a facilitator of good behaviour. Make him want to do the right thing. At all times. Not just when someone is watching.

Our children notice how we treat our family, friends, staff, pets and even beggars on the streets. **Kindness, politeness, responsibility, compassion and empathy** has to start with you. These are values which are slowly getting lost, and the world needs them more than ever today. These are both character traits and social skills, which are picked up by the child as he watches the parents practice them.

But don't demean your children in the name of teaching them etiquettes. I have seen parents are quick to remind their children to say 'goodbye' to guests, before they themselves have said it. I have seen parents admonishing their children even before they have got a gift with a, 'What do you say when you get a gift?' Give them a moment. Don't force it down their throat, lead them to it without using an insulting tone.

Express clearly the values you want your children to imbibe. Pepper your own conversations with 'thank you', 'please' and 'sorry'. If they grow up watching this, they will learn it. Responsibility for siblings, the pets, their homework, their cycle, their books, their rooms has to be inculcated slowly, over time. With reminders and soft nudges.

Empathy is the cornerstone of morality. Feel for the other, and you will never want to hurt them. Reverence for life and human values has to come from within, and it's awareness starts at home.

Show, don't just tell, in small ways how you can make the world a better place. **Encourage giving.** Maybe your child can tutor the gardener's child who needs help with Maths, or maybe you can ask them to give a stationery set to the maid's child.

When my daughter was five-years-old, she was invited for a friend's birthday party. The invite read, 'No gifts please, but there's a donation box for an NGO in case you wish to contribute.' We explained the concept of charity for the needy to her, and told her that if she could give her piggy bank along with the savings in it, it would make some needy child somewhere very happy. It was not easy for her to part with her favourite piggy bank, but she agreed.

Thirteen years later she still remembers it as her first act of charity.

Showing **gentleness** to the poor, the elderly and animals also has to be inculcated by example. Do not be rough, or tolerate roughness, from anyone. Ever see anyone kicking a stray dog on the road? Do not ignore. Stop and intervene. It is worth your time. Stranger yelling at his old father in a park? Get involved. Shame him. But don't walk away thinking, 'Not my business.' It is. Let's make it our business to create a more humane world around us.

Encourage the **courage** of showing vulnerability, grief and fear. Hiding these feelings from the children and pretending to be strong in times of distress, uncertainty and crisis will only deepen their belief that expressing these feelings is unacceptable. Share stories of your struggle and imperfections with them, and let them accept faults and mistakes as part of life and living.

Teach them, above all, to honour **hard work**, diligent toil and dignity of labour. No work is great or small, not everyone can do work which will change the world. But true greatness is doing your work with **honesty** and **sincerity**.

Communicate clearly about the importance of having good values, and your expectation from your child. Spell it out. When you keep quiet on seeing your child selfishly eating the last piece of chocolate while the younger brother cries, you are clearly sending out a message of the acceptability of selfish behaviour.

Encourage repair and amends. They won't always stick to the straight and narrow path. But when they do weaken and falter, be there to guide them. Be there to love them, and reinforce that mistakes happen, but they have to be mended. Implore them to reflect on their slip-ups, but resist the urge to punish them, or prophesy doom. A permanent behavioural change can come only through self-realization, not coercion.

Encourage them to learn one musical instrument and one sport really well. Music is a balm to the soul. It soothes the human spirit, and provides an outlet for feelings. It offers us a chance to stay emotionally healthy. To learn how to play a musical instrument requires practice, sincerity and an ear for music. Encourage them to enjoy while they learn, else this too will be reduced to a chore.

Sports are an important way to stay physically healthy. They also provide a good learning in the sportsman spirit. The rush of adrenaline along with physical exercise has been known to lead to improved social and motor skill. It teaches them the importance of values such as honesty, team work, fair play, respect for self and others and adherence to rules. It also teaches them to deal with competition, and to handle both winning and losing.

□

Where we go Wrong, as Parents

The term 'generation gap' refers to the distance in understanding and sensibility between two generations. Each generation brings the society a couple of steps ahead from where it's parents left it. The generation which grew up in pre-partition India raised the first generation of free India. Their challenges and mindsets were different. That generation of women in 1950s and 1960s, who had grown up seeing only their brothers and sons educated, started encouraging their daughters to go to school and seek formal education. This was Generation W. They supported their daughters' decision to have a career while they looked after these daughters' children. Times were changing. Gen X referred broadly to everyone born before 1990, and Gen Y is the one born after 1990.

This meant that while Gen X was busy pursuing their careers, Gen Y may have been raised by Gen W. This made bridging the generation gap between parent and child even tougher. A child brought up by his grandmother may have trouble relating to his mother, just as the mother will have trouble relating to him.

A glimpse of the sociological milieu is important to understand that wiring of Gen X and Gen Y is different. Not only in terms of thinking, priorities and values, but also in lifestyles. Since our society shifted from agricultural (1950s and 1960s) to industrial (1970s and 1980s) and now to technological (post-1990s), the world has become smaller. With computers and Internet, knowledge about what is happening in the rest of the world is now freely available. Satellite television and Internet have given our children an idea of what is happening in the world. These serve as aspirational ('this is what I'd like to buy') educational ('let's try kissing the way the actors in English serials do') easily accessible (especially porn sites). This has become a part of our lives. We cannot ignore it.

Modes of communication have been increasing, but communication itself is becoming impossible. Parents and children came from different planets, unable to understand the other's language.

Introspection and observation will tell us where we need to change and unless we are aware of our shortcomings, there's not much we'll be able to do to bring about long-term changes.

The first among these is our obsession with *donning the teacher's hat.* The impulse to teach our children is very strong. The first instinct of a parent on listening to anything his child says is to use this as a learning opportunity, a lesson. But this is like looking through the wrong end of the telescope. The best way a parent can facilitate learning is to encourage curiosity, in such a way that though thirst to know is kindled, but he is not forced to learn.

We want to teach. But we are not interested in learning as a two-way process.

Parents are the first role models for the children. So, the responsibility rests on the parents' shoulders of providing them with a suitable ideal to aspire towards.

Our children are growing and learning every day, are we? Are we? When was the last time you learnt something new? A new skill, a new sport, or a new hobby? *When was the last time you did something for the first time?*

Let's take a look at this scenario:

A five-year-old respects his parents, his first heroes are his parents; his parents know everything, they have all the answers to his questions, they are big and strong, they are capable and intelligent. They provide for him, look after him and protect him. His father can pick him up and swing him, he teaches him to play cricket and badminton, takes him swimming and teaches him the different strokes, teaches him cycling and rebukes him when he falls down and grazes his knee. His hero-worship knows no bounds.

Then what changes when the same child turns 15?

Now, the parent doesn't have all the answers. Consider the Law of Nature – from ages 30-45, father doesn't show much growth, neither mental nor physical. In fact, if anything, the father loses muscle and hair, and probably gains weight. He doesn't look as strong to his son as he looked when he was 30. He probably hasn't learnt any new skills or hobby, he hasn't kept up with the latest in the field of technology, he cannot swing his son anymore, cannot lift him up or play horse to him. He probably loses any game of badminton or cricket he plays with his son. However, from the age of 5-15, the child grows, both mentally and physically; he gains height, puts on weight, adds muscle and is capable of finding the answers to his questions on his own.

The father has slowed down, but the son has accelerated the speed on his growth.

Now, it becomes a challenge for him to respect his father in the same way.

Without realizing we fall into the familiar and comforting patterns of behaviour and routine. The new and challenging doesn't attract us anymore. We stop growing.

And this is where we have to make an extra effort. Learning new things should never cease.

Parenting should be relaxed, not pressured. It has to be enjoyed and not taken as a chore. If we, as parents, remain in a pleasant frame of mind, we will radiate that calm. If we are anxious and tense, our children will become only more so. *A happy person expands, an unhappy person contracts.* Expansion will make us inclusive, we will open our arms and hearts, but if we are unhappy we will become restricted only to ourselves. Constricted, selfish and narrow.

Every parent, and especially every successful person has a responsibility to be happy else you're setting up a bad example.

It then becomes our duty to be happy.

But it is important that our *happiness is not parasitic happiness* – dependent on others, dependent on achievements, coming with a list of, 'terms and conditions apply'! No. We have to learn to remain happy in ourselves. By learning, by growing and setting up new challenges and milestones for ourselves.

Find sustainable ways to nurture the sunny in your nature. You can't give cheerful vibes, if you yourself are running on 'empty.' You can't act much nicer than you feel.

The secret mantra here is: *Improve what you lack, enjoy what you have.*

Children have to be viewed as human beings, but we start seeing them as assets. Then we expect RoI (Return on Investment) from them! We can't monetize the investment of time and money we make on our children. They are subjects of enduring value, don't put a price tag on them!

Patterns are slippery roads. And we start sliding down the slippery roads of pre-established habits and patterns of behaviour.

The most common reason for this is fear. Fear of change, fear of the unfamiliar.

It is important not to transfer our *fears and insecurities* on to the children. It is important to make them aware, but not appropriate to stop them from doing something because you failed at it. As parents, we can teach them to look both ways before crossing the road, but out of our fear of accident, we cannot stop them from going out. *If we try and control them in every way, we will bring up children who are no better than us.*

Parents are constantly worried about not paying enough attention to their children. But here too we need to ask ourselves if we aren't making the mistake of paying *too much* attention. When it comes to attention, you have to draw a line with, 'How much is too much?'

Another big debate raging in our minds is compensating for our guilt. And what do we do? We get them gifts, give them money or increase their allowance.

Cash parenting is the worst kind of bribe that children grow up with. Guilt due to lack of time for children often is compensated with money and gifts. However, it is a wasted effort, since no gift, no matter how expensive it is, can make up for a parent's absence. We have become a very busy generation of parents, and often, we resort to shortcuts. It starts with the parents' attempt to compensate the lack of time, and later the children start taking advantage of this guilt to get the parents to buy them what they otherwise wouldn't.

Soon they know the price of everything, the value of nothing. But presents can never take the place of presence.

And we blame our children for it. But who's responsible?

Even the current malaise of, "brand consciousness", also starts with us. Since branding *awareness* starts with us. Right from the time when we start looking for a school for our children. Schools are a brand today, aren't they? Then we blame them that they only want a certain brand of clothes, gadgets or footwear! Isn't that what they see us doing? How can they do anything else?

Financial Management

Money doesn't Grow on Trees

Sensible money handling is one of life's most important skills, and yet most parents don't teach this to their children consciously. For some families, it is a taboo topic. The thinking being, 'Why trouble them with money worries from now only?'

But, like the birds-and-bees issue, this one needs to be dealt with. We should be comfortable talking about it, without arguing, in front of children, otherwise they'll view money as a stressor.

Teaching about the value and management of money should start as early as possible. Right from the time they are old enough to handle a piggy bank, they should be encouraged to save pennies.

The first critical lesson is to teach them to differentiate between *wants* and *needs*.

Talk about money choices, prioritizing needs and spending on the immediate ones. The saving-spending ratio should also be clearly explained. We cannot learn this without someone telling us how it is done. Learning by trial and error may prove to be very costly.

It Takes Money to Make Money

Fancy cars, shiny gizmos, branded clothing, foreign trips and private jets are good to fantasize about, but the importance of money earned through hard and honest work has to be underlined. *Inherited money, or the expectation of it, should not stop children from making an honest living themselves.*

Financial lessons have to be taught and reinforced every day. A good way to do this is to talk aloud when you are making financial decisions so they can listen: "Do we really need to buy an air conditioner from this shop, or should we check out some discounts on shopping sites also?" "Can we go to the amusement park next month since we're already going out for dinner this week?" "Should we buy a car this year since we've already booked a foreign trip?"

When children are a little older, say around 16-17-years old, it is important to explain to them that money has to be clearly put under four heads:

Save, spend, donate and *invest*.

Explain the ratio of each head separately, and the need to stick to it.

Monthly pocket allowance should be fixed, and the expenditure heads should be clarified by the parents. List each item clearly which the child has to cover in the allowance – like clothes, eating out, gifts, parties, mobile and petrol bills.

Another excellent habit is to get them to maintain a *financial journal* or ledger where they list their expenses. This is a great way to make them realize where their money is going, and to channelize it, if need be, into the more important areas.

Help your child to prepare a wish list for his savings. It will give him an added incentive to save. make him write down in his journal, clearly:

- What he's saving for?
- How long it will take him to reach his savings goal.

With a clear wish list in mind, the next step is to teach him to save. Saving starts with cutting down on extra expenses. And investing the savings to reach the saving goal quicker. If it is a big item, like a cellphone, a car or a foreign trip, it is a good idea to suggest how much you will contribute to the savings fund, and how he can space out his savings to reach his goal. Suggest different savings plan for different timeline schedules. For instance, if your 15-year old wants to save ₹ 20,000 for her cellphone, and her monthly allowance is ₹ 5000, tell her that if she wants to buy the cellphone in four months' time, she will have to save her entire allowance for those four months. With ₹ 1000 savings per month, it will take her almost two years to reach her target, and so on.

It is an important life lesson, in that they learn to delay gratification, they learn that they have to wait to buy something big and also that they have to be ready to sacrifice something in order to get something big. This also teaches them that needs cannot be fulfilled instantly, that patience is an important aspect of realizing our targets, and that we have to work towards achieving our desires. The whole process of saving, then getting what they want will also make them realize the value of what they have, and they will be extra cautious in handling it.

Because easy come, is easy go.

Planning School Holidays

School holidays are opportunities for parents to be with their children. Let's not waste them by letting them sit in front of the TV or computer screens, or pushing them from one class to the other, while we carry on with our lives as usual.

Here too, the first and foremost thing is to put *yourself*, the parent, into the school holiday mode. Do not pack their days with too many classes.

Relaxation, even getting bored, is important for them. It is a good time to learn a new skill or hobby, but what is more important is to make it fun for them. Some suggestions are as follows.

Exercise Together

One thing which is common across all classes and strata of society is that this generation is just not stepping out enough. They want to join health clubs and gyms, granted, but they're not getting out and playing, climbing trees, chasing butterflies, cycling, or even meeting the neighbours. Traffic in metros doesn't permit them to run about unattended, and we don't find the time to take them to parks. As a result, this generation is growing up indoors.

Children need fresh air and exercise. We all do. And holidays are a good time to encourage activities related to physical fitness, preferably in open air and sunshine. Cycling, jogging, swimming, basketball, cricket, family picnics, etc. are just some of the activities which can be fun. *Parks, playgrounds and picnics* should feature in the holiday schedule in a big way.

But the catch here is that parents need to get outside, too. The upside is that along with good health, you also get to make beautiful memories and get your family back in sync. These family fun activities are what the children will look back and remember all their lives.

Join some sport, like badminton or basketball, and make sure you play too. Going to a club or the nearest sports academy can become a family activity. And, how about swimming? If you haven't learnt it yet, now is as good a time as any.

Play Board Games, Get Arty and Crafty

Games like Monopoly, Scrabble, Jenga, Brainvita, Pictionary, Cluedo, Chess, Carromboard, Upwords and Lego are fun and a good learning tool. For long, hot summer afternoons, there's nothing like a good board game with the family!

There are also art and craft kits which teach painting, making masks, pottery, knitting, bead weaving, tile and mosaic paintings, sand art, Scooby string making and many, many more. Get creative and get involved while the children craft new things. Does a hedge or the flower pots need a fresh coat of paint? Well, now's the time to get the children to do it. Do not be a stickler for perfection here. Don't worry too much if it doesn't look perfect. Enjoy the process more than the cleaning up you'll have to do. Trust me, it is as good for you as it is for them.

Story-telling and Reading

We are never too old to listen to stories. This is a fact. Pull down the books you've been meaning to read to them, or wishing they would read themselves. This is also the right time to take them to a book store or the neighbourhood library, and let them pick out the books they want to read in the holidays, with some suggestions from you. There are some books which are a must-read. Make a list of them according to the age at which they should be read, and suggest accordingly.

Catch up on Movies

Like some books, even a few movies are a must-watch. Catch up on them with the children. Postpone household chores for a while. Microwave a bowl of popcorn, and settle down with the children in front of the TV and enjoy this perk of parenthood.

Get Them to Help you in Cooking

And introduce them to the basics of cooking. Keeping their age in mind, you can teach them how to make rotis, omelette, and some basic vegetables. It is an important skill, and has to be introduced from a young age to make the children self-reliant. Younger kids can be asked to lay the table, or peel boiled potatoes. You can introduce the nutritional information as you cook, and this will encourage them to choose healthy food as a matter of habit. Or you can tempt them by asking them to choose a dish they want to eat, and cook it with their help, step by step. Baking with kids is also a fun activity, and they will enjoy the taste as well the aroma of freshly baked cookies which they helped their Mom prepare.

However, keep in mind that you do this when you are neither stressed, nor on a tight schedule. Try not to be annoyed if things get messy or the peeling and cooking is not up to the mark. They will pick up the skill to do it right. Have patience. And, meanwhile, remember to thank them for their assistance.

Volunteer Time for Some Social Service, or Help a Neighbour

The neighbourhood library needs help to catalogue their books? The nearby School for the Blind wants to upload audio books? The local orphanage wants to computerize its records? Ask around for places which are child-friendly, and will appreciate voluntary services. Then introduce your child to the pleasure of volunteering time for social service.

The neighbour wants help mowing his lawn, or walking his dog? Suggest to your children that they might want to help. When we offer selfless service, with nothing in return, it is extremely satisfying. And goes a long way in character building.

Connect with the Extended Family

Now is the time to visit the grandparents, uncles, aunts and cousins. Not very long back, summer holidays meant going and staying at the maternal grandparents' house. All the cousins got together at the *Nani House,* and bonded over shared meals, tree climbing, cycling and playing pranks on the neighbours! It is a nice idea to plan picnics and outings with the extended family, and get the cousins to spend time together. This will not only forge healthy family bonds, but will also foster emotional health by providing the social connect which we all crave.

Introduce the Pleasure of Gardening

This summer get your children to grow green fingers. If you don't have a garden, teach them how to grow plants, may be fresh herbs, in pots. It's a nice idea to teach them science through gardening. Introduce the names of the plants and trees to them. Tell them the basics of life in plants. Get them to plant a sapling, call it by the child's name, and tell him it's his responsibility to look after that plant and make sure it thrives. Teach them the right way of watering and weeding. Get them to dirty their hands in soil. Connect them to mother earth.

Involve them in Holiday Planning

This would mean planning an itinerary, looking up discounts and deals and hotel bookings. Extensive research is required, but it is all available if one has the patience and a little guidance. Get them to decide which place they want to visit, give them a set budget and ask them to plan a vacation. They can decide everything from mode of transportation to whether it should be a standard or luxury room, the sightseeing attractions in those places and the price of the tickets. Ask them to factor in unforeseen expenses. Once it is done, thrash down the last detail with them.

Children will have more fun when you go for a holiday they planned. Plan a surprise or two for them, like a trip to the amusement park they cut out because of budgetary constraints. After all, holidays are all about being fun and spontaneous. One child can become the official holiday photographer, while the other can be asked to maintain a holiday journal. Don't fret over pennies, but keep the children involved in the budget. If you're going overboard, cut down an activity or dinner in a fancy restaurant. If you're within, or below your spending limit, splurge on mementos or gifts before you return home.

Handling Rebellion – Behaviour Triggered by Rebellion

This is a part of growing up. And is not to be confused with a lifelong behavioural aberration. All children rebel. The strong-willed rebel just a little more. The expression differs: from tattoos, body piercings, long hair, messy rooms, grunge jeans and hippie unkempt look. And the stronger willed they are, the more power struggles there are going to be.

But all this is a phase in their growing up. It is a part of defining and discovering their individuality. It is an important step on the path of self-discovery. They are not being difficult on purpose to annoy you, they dislike being told what to do. Ultimately, it boils down to your expectation of complete and unquestioning obedience from them.

Forcing obedience on your child and breaking his spirit by punishment will have far more serious consequences in his later life since he will become readily vulnerable to negative figures of authority, ready to do what he is told.

Is that what you want?

The way to handle it right is to take a deep breath and see it from their context. If it is not harming their life or health, draw a line and let them figure out how to stay within the boundary and express their individuality. Try to empathize, set down some ground rules and reinforce that respect goes both ways. Listen to their point of view in a non-judgmental way. Maybe he's not rebelling, maybe he's just upset. Try meeting him half way. If she insists on wearing a short dress to a family function and you think it is inappropriate, ask her to consider teaming it up with stockings. Or maybe, she could save that dress for the dinner at that fancy restaurant you are planning to take her to later in the week.

If you give orders, he will resist. If you give choices, he will feel he is still in control of his life. But give choices that *you*, the parent, can live with. 'No body piercing, but you can get a tattoo,' should not be followed by constant nagging about how ugly the tattoo looks!

Don't push him into opposing you, don't give ultimatums or threats. Else he will have no choice but to defy you. Every punishment and threat puts another brick in the wall that our child builds with us, and it becomes very difficult to dismantle this wall. Everything doesn't have to be a battle, and if you think it is, and you want to win every battle with him, remember this: even if you win the battle, you will lose your relationship with your child.

Is it worth it?

More importantly, refrain from issuing orders, and saying things like, 'just because I say so.' Don't attend every power struggle you are invited to. Step back. Do not scream, yell, or throw a fit. Don't let your teen make you behave a five-year-old!

There are some parents, figures I've come across in books which have taught me a thing or two about parenting. I want to share these here.

Atticus Finch as a Parenting Model

To Kill a Mockingbird

The best fictional parenting model I ever came across was Atticus Finch. He doesn't preach, he teaches by example. His stern but fair attitude towards his children, Jem and Scout, reaches into the courtroom as well. He lives by his conscience, and has a strong character. When his daughter Scout tells him that most people in the town think it's wrong to defend the black man accused of rape, Atticus explains that "They're entitled to full respect for their opinions. But before I can live with other folks I've got to live with myself. The one thing that doesn't abide by majority rule is a person's conscience."

He reinforces the importance of looking at both sides of the story. When our children are throwing a tantrum and we start getting angry at them, perhaps it would be better to look at the situation from their viewpoint, as Atticus inspired me to do after I re-read this book again after becoming a parent.

The biggest lesson he gives his children is his faith in justice and the judicial system. He knows before the trial begins that he's going to lose this case, but that doesn't stop him from giving his best because he knows that the accused, Tom, an African American, is innocent.

Another important lesson is being, totally honest with your children. Even with the difficult questions. He believes that honesty will breed honesty, and children are quick to spot when you are lying or withholding information from them. The best example is when 8-year-old Scout asks him what "rape" means, Atticus gives her a dry, but accurate, legal definition without going into the physical details, or telling her, 'you are too young to understand.'

Tiger Mother

Amy Chua coined the term 'Tiger Mother' is a book to mean a mother who is a strict disciplinarian. This book describes her efforts to give her children a traditional, strict "Chinese" upbringing. Chua explains the essential differences between Western and Chinese parents. She says that Western parents think children know what's best for themselves and they let their children become independent with decision-making from a fairly young age. Whereas Chinese parents believe that their children owe them everything and that they, as parents, know what is best for their children, even if that means overriding their children's natural skills and preferences.

In one example, Chua mentioned that she had called one of her children 'garbage', Chua described how she got her unwilling younger daughter to learn a very difficult piano piece, telling her to stop being lazy, cowardly, self-indulgent and pathetic. She even forbade her daughter at this time to, "get up, not for water, not even for bathroom breaks."

Her Chinese methods seem a little extreme to Indian parents, but a happy mix of both the parenting styles could work better.

Helicopter Parents

This is now a widely acknowledged style of parenting, where the parents keep 'hovering' around the child at all times. These parents are overfocused on every aspect of their children's life: what they are eating, how many hours they are studying, who are they playing with, why are they getting low grades? They take on too much responsibility, and end up over-controlling every aspect of their child's lives. Doing tasks for them which they are physically and mentally capable of doing for themselves. Like tying the shoelaces, carrying their school bags, monitoring their day-to-day school activity, calling up teachers to question them about grades, calling up friends to cross check and many more of such controlling habits. The consequence of this style of parenting is children who are emotionally dependent, have low self-esteem and confidence, and undeveloped coping and other life skills. They lack decisiveness, and look to the parents to make decisions for them and solve their issues.

As a parent, the task before us is to tread the fine line between being there for our child, but letting him make his decisions. This line will keep shifting each day, decreasing your area and increasing his area of control and decision making regarding his life. It is not going to be easy watching him make mistakes which you know you can avert. But it is important if we want to raise self-reliant kids.

Their behaviour, their confidence and self-reliance will reflect how successful you've been at it.

Bringing up Have-lots

The challenges of this generation of children which is growing up in abundance are different from the earlier generation. About 50 years back, frugal spending, simple living and sensible saving was the motto. Now, with plastic money, EMIs and easy loans ensure that postponement is just not necessary. One can get what one wants now.

As a result, this generation is growing up *expecting* that it is the parents' duty to fulfil every demand of the children. There is no end to the latest gadgets, phones, games, cars, clothes and shoes. Marketing companies target the children in their advertisements because they know the real movers are the children of the family! Social pressure does the rest of the work.

The line between need and greed is getting blurred.

If kids today feel like this, it is because we're raising them in a culture of acquisition and consumption, of accumulating rather than sharing, of owning rather than giving. Partly, it is because of us. Because when they want connect and emotional nurture, we give them stuff. To help kids change, we have to examine our own lives and assumptions first.

Sensible and responsible parenting can manage this issue, but there are a few more tips which can come in handy.

Be a Suitable Role Model

Here again, it is up to us to foster attitudes in our children. If they see us splurging unnecessarily, or shopping for the 'feel-good' factor, so will our children. If you "must have" the latest model of your favourite brand of handbag, your child will do the same. Alternately, if you practice sensible and prioritized shopping, coupled with gratitude for everything you have, so will your child.

Don't Substitute Presents with Presence

When we feel guilty that we aren't spending

enough time with our kids, we buy them things. We increase their allowance. We give 'stuff' which is possible for us to give them. But, not our time. When children get demanding and expect us to get what and when they demand it, it is time to consider where our parenting needs to be tweaked. Emotional needs are satisfied by emotional closeness, not material things which can be bought off the shelf of a supermarket.

Empower Kids to Create Their Own Abundance

What is your most common response when your child asks you for a new computer game? Or phone?

"Don't even think about it. Do you think money grows on trees? First learn to take care of the things you have."

Didn't we just shame the child? We told him he is unworthy of getting a new game, that he is greedy for wanting another when he already has one, that he is careless about his stuff, and that he is stupid if he thinks it is easy to earn money.

Phew! That's a lot of insults for wanting something.

And, we all want something or the other, all the time.

How about this?

"I can get it if you promise you'll be a good boy and finish your homework by yourself?"

This is bribing. Plain and simple. This will send the message that it is okay to make false promises if you want something, that if you make a fuss you get anything you want. This purchase will soon lose its attraction since it was too easy, then he'll manipulate you for the next one. It will foster the habit of acquiring more without feeling gratitude for what he has, both material and non-material.

Another option?

"You really want that? Oh!, your friend Arvind got it last week as his birthday present? Do you want me to put it on your birthday list? Your birthday is a long way off, I know. But this is not on our list of expenses for now. So, let's schedule it for later."

This child knows it is not an outright rejection of his wish. He knows now that he can get it, eventually. That wants have to be prioritized, too.

Money has to be earned with hard and sincere work. If the father wants to leave money to his children, fine. But this should be no reason to not work. Also, we have to make sure that they respect labour, and do not think any work is too small for them, or beneath their position.

Enforce Dignity of Labour and the Importance of Hard Work

It is easy to fall into the vicious cycle of entitlement and inheritance. When children see the family wealth, they grow up feeling it is their right to inherit the family assets and money. After all, isn't that what the father is working so hard for? So that his kids can lead a comfortable life, without having to slog for it? But, this is a defeatist pattern of thinking, and should be nipped in the bud.

Mitigate the Harmful Effects of Advertising

As a marketing gimmick, advertisements show that happiness can be bought. You buy the best microwave, and hey! Your family is smiling. Stuck in the heat? Buy the latest brand of air conditioner and your entire family will be dancing with joy.

In the child's mind, the message received is that possessions = happiness. That happiness can be bought. That the more things you buy, the more happy you will be.

Explain to the child that buying is an addiction, and material things can never give us true happiness. Live this philosophy with sincerity. And sooner or later, the children will start living it too.

Show them that what matters the most to you is the people you love. Working hard. Following your passion. Giving back to society. Tell them these things in clear words. They'll understand then that life holds abundance beyond accumulating material possessions.

Teach Them to be Responsible for Their Damaged Goods

It is a good idea to let the child pay for something he has lost or broken from his pocket allowance. Everything from a broken phone to lost school books, misplaced shoes and computer games. This sends out a powerful message about valuing what they have, and stepping up and taking responsibility.

Practice Donations and Charity

Out of 24 hours in a day, we should spend at least 24 minutes doing something selfless, for someone who needs it more importantly. Give your child the opportunity to discover how good it feels to help others. What can kids do? There are a lot of options, depending on their age. They can volunteer time at the neighborhood library, join the NGO which needs help with teaching poor children, or they can teach the maid's children at home. The idea is to promote selfless service.

Giving will make them understand that hoarding can never give us true happiness.

□□□